By John Wieners

The Hotel Wentley Poems (1958)
Of Asphodel, In Hell's Despite (1963)
Ace of Pentacles (1964)
Chinoiserie (1965)
Pressed Wafer (1967)
A Letter to Charles Olson (1968)
Asylum Poems (1969)
Youth (1970)
Nerves (1970)
Selected Poems (1972)
Playboy (1972)
Woman (1972)
The Lanterns Along the Wall (1972)
Hotels (1974)
Behind the State Capitol (1975)
Selected Poems: 1958–1984 (1986)

JOHN WIENERS

CULTURAL AFFAIRS IN BOSTON: POETRY & PROSE 1956-1985

Edited by Raymond Foye

Preface by Robert Creeley

BLACK SPARROW PRESS / SANTA ROSA / 1988

Grateful acknowledgement is made to the following institutions for the use of materials in their collections: The Bancroft Library, University of California, Berkeley; The Poetry/Rare Books Collection, SUNY/Buffalo; The Archive for New Poetry, University of California, San Diego; The Frank Melville, Jr. Memorial Library, SUNY/Stony Brook; The Fales Collection, New York University. The author wishes to acknowledge the generosity of the John Simon Guggenheim Foundation, the National Endowment for the Arts, and the Foundation for Contemporary Performing Arts.

LIBRARY OF CONGRESS CATALOGING-IN-PUBLICATION DATA

Wieners, John, 1934–
    Cultural Affairs in Boston : poetry & prose, 1956-1985 / John Wieners ; edited by Raymond Foye ; preface by Robert Creeley.
        p.   cm.
    Includes index.
ISBN 0-87685-739-X :   ISBN 0-87685-738-1 (pbk.) :
ISBN 0-87685-740-3 (signed) :
    I. Foye, Raymond, 1957-   . II. Title.
PS3573.I35C85   1988
811'.54—dc19   88-21550
                                        CIP

for Charles Shively

Table of Contents

Preface

The poetry of John Wieners has an exceptionally human beauty—as if there ever were any other. There is in it such a commonness of phrase and term, such a substantial fact of a daily life transformed by the articulateness of his feelings and the intensity of the inexorable world that is forever out there waiting for any one of us. Charles Olson spoke of it as "a poetry of affect," by which I took him to mean a poetry that is in the process of a life being lived, literally, as Keats' was, or Hart Crane's, or Olson's own. In other words, the art becomes the complex act of "making real" all that one is given to live, and whatever in them may be style or fashion, the poems are so otherwise committed, so intensely a gesture of primary need and recognition, that their survival becomes the singular value, and their immense beauty.

In the brutal outrage of the late 1950's, when one could pick up a Government bulletin on the home manufacture of a bomb shelter at the post office, Mr. Wieners' painful survival in words became our own: "At last. I come to the last defense." There was nothing else to shelter or protect him. Time and again during the 60's one wondered, worried, whether he could make it. How specious such simply charitable impulse looks in retrospect. He *was* there, he *stayed* there—as Charles Olson once said, "he's *elemental*." His writing of this time is various, often magnificent, ringing curious changes on Augustan patterns. But whatever one would hope so to qualify becomes unequivocally clear in "The Acts of Youth," that great poem of life's implacable realities and the will committed to suffer them.

If poetry might be taken as a distance, some space from the action, relief from the crowd, or if its discretions, what it managed to leave out, avoid, get rid of, were its virtue, then all these poems would be in one way or another suspect. They are far closer to a purported Chinese apothegm I read years ago and continue to muse on: "How is it far if you think it?" I don't truly know. It doesn't seem to be far at all. Nor do these poems, any of them, seem ever some place else, or where they move apart from an agent, either feeling or thinking. They're here, as we are—certainly a hopeful convention in all respects, but where else to meet?

The present collection is, then, an intense respect of this fact, and the range of its materials—three decades of poetry and prose—

11

makes manifest the complex place from which all John Wieners' work finally has come, and to which it, as he also, insistently returns: "my city, Boston . . ." He said once to an interviewer, "I am a Boston poet," and there is no one for whom that city, or any other, has proved so determining and generative an experience. The changing faces of its presence and persons become articulate here in this dear man's immaculate art. Against the casual waste of our usual lives, his has proved a cost and commitment so remarkable. He has given everything to our common world.

We read together years ago at the 92nd Street Y in New York, with its great velvet curtain, raised stage. John remembered hearing Auden read there and was moved that now we would. He was thrilled that one might so follow, and so we did. But now, in these times so bitterly without human presence, risk, care, response, he becomes the consummate artist of our common voice, and his battered, singular presence our own.

Robert Creeley

Introduction

Raymond Foye: A Visit with John Wieners

Our interview took place over the Christmas holiday, 1984. Mr. Wieners' apartment on Joy Street in Boston was gaily decorated for the season, with styrofoam reindeer, Santa Clauses, twinkling candles, elves made from red and green felt, and a plastic nativity scene perched atop the portable T.V. set in a corner of the bedroom. This is the same suite of rooms the poet has occupied for twelve years, and he tells visitors that he derives great pleasure from this corner of historic Beacon Hill. His three rooms are sparsely furnished. There is a front sitting room, a back bedroom where he sleeps and writes, and a guest bedroom. There are several bookcases but they are all empty. Old movie magazines and 1950s detective pulps collect on his bedside table, next to a copy of *Beyond Beauty* by Arlene Dahl. On the coffeetable in the front room Mr. Wieners has placed a black folio containing all of his work from the past two years.

A delicate porcelain Chinese bowl also sits on the table, filled to the brim with aspirin tablets, "for the guests," he explains. But Mr. Wieners is a genial host, and offers the pick of a bountiful cheese and fruit basket his sister Marion has sent for the holidays. Throughout the interview he smoked incessantly, but spoke in a relaxed manner. He occasionally rose to pace the room, or stood gazing out the window at the snowfall that had begun to dust the gold dome of the state capitol building.

At one point the phone rang, and it was his good friend Charles Shively, extending a dinner invitation in Cambridge that evening, which he accepted for both of us. Shively remains one of the few friends Wieners stays in touch with, and he has been a valued secretary, editor and publisher since the early seventies.

Mr. Wieners was eager for news of New York, and hoped to make his yearly visit over the New Year's. He asked about the repairs being made on St. Mark's Church, and inquired about a recent Cy Twombly exhibition. As we settled down to this interview, he turned on the radio, fiddled briefly with the dial, and found Billie Holiday singing "The Man I Love." The transcript captures some of the quixotic nature of his conversation, some of his wry

13

and pithy delivery, but remains only a scanty residuum of any encounter with this rare poet, where the best is always left unsaid.

RAYMOND FOYE: What made up your mind to attend Black Mountain College?

JOHN WIENERS: They sent me train fare.

RF: Recently I was reading some of your juvenilia, poems written as a student at Black Mountain.

WIENERS: Those were not supposed to be published.

RF: I was surprised to find you writing in a very long line— Whitmanesque. Because your first book, *The Hotel Wentley Poems*, is exceedingly spare. What precipitated that shift?

WIENERS: I was starving, so I wrote lean poems.

RF: Were you living at the Hotel Wentley?

WIENERS: For a summer. And hanging out in Bob's room. (La Vigne—RF.)

RF: Was he away?

WIENERS: No, he was there.

RF: It seems to have been a productive period.

WIENERS: Not really, I was reading, mostly, and watching Bob paint. It's hard to remember the follies of one's youth.

RF: Do you ever miss San Francisco?

WIENERS: Not a day goes by that I don't think of it.

RF: I noticed some tiny maps on your bedroom wall, of San Francisco, of Buffalo . . .

WIENERS: It's funny how these cities die when we leave them.

RF: Who are the early influences on your poetry?

WIENERS: Edna St. Vincent Millay was the first. Later it was Charles Olson.

RF: And at the time of the *Wentley* poems?

WIENERS: Olson, until 1973.

RF: And who since then?

14

WIENERS: The Virgin Mary.

RF: There aren't many books here, but I notice you're reading Melville.

WIENERS: He must have been wonderful company in those wooden frame houses!

RF: I also saw the memoirs of Blaze Starr . . .

WIENERS: . . . from which I'm borrowing heavily for my own autobiography.

RF: In assembling your *Collected Poems*, you've been reluctant to reprint much of your early work.

WIENERS: They're old faces I don't care to see again.

RF: You've always spoken to me quite highly of Robert Creeley's work.

WIENERS: Oh yes, I'm mad about obtuseness!

RF: I once saw a photograph of you, walking in San Marco in Venice, between Olson and Ezra Pound. Rather exalted company.

WIENERS: To say the least.

RF: What was Pound like?

WIENERS: Oh, he was a mama's boy.

RF: You once recommended to me translation, as a valuable exercise for a poet.

WIENERS: In teaching *contrapunctus.*

RF: Can we talk about writing poetry?

WIENERS: I'm just the co-pilot.

RF: Do you have a theory of poetics?

WIENERS: I try to write the most embarrassing thing I can think of.

RF: Have you ever been bored by your great technical facility?

WIENERS: Yes.

RF: Have you a preferred working method?

WIENERS: Confusion, usually.

RF: Until the age of thirty-five, you were quite prolific as a poet, but as time went on, you wrote less and less.

WIENERS: When I first wrote poetry it was out of a need for personal expression. But as one works it's inevitable that one becomes more self-conscious, and it's so easy to slip into self-indulgence. And then the spontaneity begins to depart.

RF: In that case it's better to stop?

WIENERS: Yes.

RF: It seems to me a major shift took place in your work, circa 1972. You abandoned the terse, lyric poems for a more hallucinative prose style—more extroverted, and decidedly political.

WIENERS: I felt I'd exhausted my subjects at that point.

RF: When I showed you what I'd assembled for the forthcoming Black Sparrow book [*Selected Poems: 1958–1984*—ed.] you were somewhat taken aback by the size of it.

WIENERS: My next book is going to consist of one word: Doris.

RF: May we consult the texts? *Selected Poems*, 1972. A poem called "Jive."

WIENERS: That's rather promiscuous.

RF: Do you remember writing each of these?

WIENERS: Oh yes.

RF: "Monday Sunrise."

WIENERS: That was written out of Bellevue. On the eighth floor. You get a marvelous view of Manhattan and the East River. Don't be afraid if you ever get sent there, it's beautiful inside.

RF: You've written several poems to painters.

WIENERS: I found them better company.

RF: Than your fellow poets?

WIENERS: Yes, they were always too vampyric.

RF: This one is to Delaunay ("The Windows").

WIENERS: It was requested by Mr. Schuyler who then worked for *Art News*. The idea was to publish poems derived from paintings.

16

At the Farnsworth Collection in the Lamont Library at Harvard I used to look at the art books. And I came across this painting, which had been given to a poet. And I thought this might tie in. I stayed for three days, trying to equate each color or gesture with a sound. It was an attempt at approximation, without reference to thought. So the poem was rejected.

RF: It was a little tenuous for *Art News*?

WIENERS: I was not capable of coherence then.

RF: Yesterday we were talking of Lacan and you seemed to take a dim view.

WIENERS: To render psychology in terms of rationality is an outrage.

RF: Do you ever tire of the literary life?

WIENERS: It never fags me.

RF: You live very much alone, here in Boston. Are you disillusioned?

WIENERS: Oh, no. It's not possible to be disillusioned. Not when one lives in the Holy Spirit.

RF: Your new poems are . . .

WIENERS: . . . scarce.

RF: Well, they're that too. I think we've typed up about thirty pages.

WIENERS: Thirty pages from a fifty-year-old in 1984 is quite a lot, I think. But I am not ready to write my last book yet. I will write it in my old age.

RF: And until then?

WIENERS: I am living out the logical conclusion of my books.

RF: Is there a poem you've yet to write?

WIENERS: I want to write a poem about an old person dying of loneliness. I want to write a poem about an old person, alone in a room, dying of hunger and loneliness. No one has ever written a poem about an old person dying in the cold, of hunger and loneliness. Except of course Ava Gardner, who is always our master.

Cultural Affairs in Boston

Poetry and Prose 1956-1985

"Hart Crane, Harry Crosby . . ."

Hart Crane, Harry Crosby, I see you going over the edge,
Hart Crane, Harry Crosby, I see you going down,
what does it feel like
to fall over
the end,
To know that you're going down and you're not coming up.
Ah Hart Crane, Crane, Harry Crosby,
don't run out on me,
stay with me with me, men,
build up my shoulderblades.
Let me carry what you threw away.
Come on, men, give me the insides of your souls.
I mean one can only cry so much,
Hart Crane, Harry Crosby,
I know you guys lived like I do,
crawling around on dirty sheets,
hoping nobody knocks on your door,
and all the time, He is knocking, beating,
let me, give me the beautiful things,
squeeze it out, pick it,

out of your hair, tell the old women under the tin roofs
that life can be better,
that love is the only value,
when the bombs break their tulips
when the shells kill their lovers,
Come on Harry, give a little,
help us, we don't want to die,
I don't want to jump out of the Ritz Tower,

Get us away from ourselves,
Bring us back to babyland, or if we only could go to sleep, Harry,
or to bed.
Oh, wipe the silver tears away,
fly the red flag of fire in our hearts, Harry.

I'll tell you one last thing,
that this is the agony you saw

coming down from your New York hotel.
This is what made you jump.

[1956]

"And what is nothingness"

And what is nothingness.
   Sometimes I see a shadow
   outside my window and that
      is nothingness.

It is the leaf of the callalilly
   plant unfolding. It is
   living at night. And looking
      into the pit of yourself

And hearing something clink
   in the silence.
            Is it junk

[1958]

San Francisco, 1958

And always these tropical songs call me
        into the south, the lush land
that I have denied long enough, the
        heat and speed, I now
        embrace, in this yellow flare
        before my eyes.
The Voice of Mexico sibilant in my ears,
        its rose along my flesh
in the drugstore window with spikes and
        needles. Point to
Vera Cruz. Prefix dans Mexicali Rose.
        Not Tonia la Negra who sings
along the sea but Nemi and Bop.
        Not the lake. Cheap
        visions and highway
        motels. Move over the
guitar strums. It leaves me
        hanging in the air
        above the border,
                of the song

[1958]

W O W
                    which is MOM spelled upside
                              down

I wanted to write a Thanksgiving poem about
   my mother how did
   she get in here and
   drunk too always on
   holidays how will I
   go about getting her
out.

   Of myself?
Where she lodges se-
curely in the loins
destroying my life
i.e. babies

   Oh well she will
go on getting drunk
in the cellar and being
carried upstairs to bed
where I will undress
her in my dreams.

[11.28.58]

2nd Communique for the Heads

I love my fellow poets.

But I do not write for them. I write for heads.
They who stick your necks up into outerspace, they who
will not allow my fingers to make a mistake on this machine, no
matter
how I falter, or err. It is all here. The periods are struck in the
furnace the same as the chains we all wear around our heads

hair.

I can do nothing but write. I starve, and have no roof over my
head
but the homes of strangers

friends who take me in. I travel everywhere. I am as air.
I am puffed up with myself as a crow. I learned this trick
from a friend.

Who is a fellow poet. Traveller.

[1958]

238 Cambridge Street: An Occasional verse

We're back on the scene
again with linoleum floors
and Billie H blowing the blues
fine & mellow it is with PG
cooking in the kitchen,
Jennifer walking through the rooms
'What are you talking about
you know you're gonna get some,'—
she says to Melly but
it ain't the same, baby,
her old man's in Mexico and
mine, mine's a square in
San Francisco while we
haunt an old city on the Atlantic
waiting in the night for a fix.

[January 6th Nativity 1959]

Poem for #238

Again camp is set up
on ruins of the old
we build anew. Drapes
brought in and dishes.
Books used to write on,
not read. Bones of dead
men we carve as chairs, rub-
bish dug out, oil bought
for the stove, blankets and
silver washed, our faces too
clean, in the morning, walls
painted and trinkets hung
to nails. We turn on then,
get high to celebrate a new
pad, place where dreams are
entertained not the enemy.
His secret ours. The long
day spent in building boats
to carry our bodies back to
God. His ancient corridors
line the walls of our flesh.

[January 7, 1959]

For the Mind of 38 Grove Street 3rd Front

Against the light
a laugh a warmth at my hip a hand
and there is
peace here in 38 Grove Street two
over from Garden 5 over from the gardens
there is a happy mouth
and poets in chairs contented
behind painted walls

I would
as they say
fain lie back into the warmth
the gas
better talking of bedrooms and pathways

On the streets papers are footsteps
men who would stab me
'to feel my warm blood over his skin'
yet eyelashes long on the red cheek
gas in the jet
brush my will.
to

I will be able to leave by morning.

[1959]

'Peyote poem'

With no fresh air in my lungs
                        in the middle of
the night, inhabited by strange gods
                                    who
are they, they walk by in white trenchcoats
    with pkgs. of paradise in their pockets.

                    Their hands.

[1959]

As Preface to Transmutations

How long ago Steve, it was
we walked along Arlington Street
throwing words to the wind.
Before junk, before jail before
we moved to the four corners
                    of the world
And you lived on Grove Street
and wrote poems poems poems
to the Navy, to Marshall, to
Boston Common. A simple life.
                    Frantic comedown.
                    Gone our lovers.
Gone Arlington, Beacon and Charles
                    Streets, Easter Sunday March
29, 1959. I look now out a back window
in San Francisco. 6 months in Danvers.
                    How can the poem
shine in your eyes in those dark cells?
Bang. Arlington Street comes down
                    with a clump.
Oh for a blade of grass.
                    Oh for a room with
                        the rent paid.
Oh for a roof.
                    I see before me the cobblestones
and the camera. Dana and you
                    in the sun ducking
out of the lens.
                    You cannot move
faster than the shutter of my mind.
                    Those old elms bend over
the street and form an arch
                    that we walk under.
Sad priests in the 20th century.
                    We began the second half
together. We chalked our words
                    on red brick
and left them for the rain.
                    It is not kind.
Nor time.

                    Nor memory the Mother.
                              A thing of barbs and
        needles. The street is long.
                              It runs to the ends
                                        of the earth.
              We are still
                on it.
                    But cannot see
                or hear the other.
                              What traffic
                              drowns out
                              all our notes.

        [1959]

                              Part II

    The traffic in the city of Boston has steadily increased, and
the national debt by 1966 will be between 7 to 8 billion dollars.
They have torn down the West End, they have torn down Scollay
Square, they have torn down nearly all of Copley Square, erecting
insurance companies, parking lots and underground garages in their
place. As a center, they have placed urban restaurants, made out
of plate glass and neon signs. Renewal they call it. Gone the elegant,
old hotels, basement cafeterias, underground jazz cellars, and strip
atheneum. All night movies, the Silver Dollar at the corner of
Boylston and Essex are dark while Nedicks shines on. Old haunts
of these poems, they become bombs to blow up in the face of the
future, they have become the future itself: BLAST; in the face of
emblems of the past we live by.
    Queen's Row is no more. Those bricks in Arlington Street,
known the world over now moulder in the city sun. The Queen's
Rosary once told by the buttons on a sailor's fly, 13 in all, is counted
no more. Instead retreated to a men's room, where for the price
of a dime, you can purchase a flea. Beacon Hill is no more, the Lin-
colnshire, where Eugene O'Neill died, is now a Nurses' Home. The
North End holds its own, but gangsterism prevalent there prevents
kind inhabitation.
    What is left? The South End, where the Poet plys his trade.
Boston has no East End, tho there is an East Boston, only the
desperate go there.
    It is here in the South End that the Poet lives, where the

outcasts of old times swing. No longer Billie Holiday at the Savoy, but Jan Balas still stumbles through the streets at dawn. No longer Malcolm X on Mass Avenue at the Roseland Ballroom (that's gone too) no longer Tremont and Boylston, they've moved out to Roxbury; oh Billy Donahue, he's underground at the Navy Yard. I thought that was Roger Weber's tramping ground. Anyway, here is Steve Jonas, here is the language he makes real, the city he lives by and that has died under his grasp, the gods he lives with, the poets he meets, and the men he has loved, and the painters, that are thrown in for good measure. Here is the poetry he makes come alive.

[1965]

On the First Page

Out my window
runs the Neponset, a river enough to be written,
(but bloody from my baby wounds).
Phlox flowers, purple for any passage
or page or poem,
(planted because Mrs. Reddington had yellow phlox).
Green grow the oak trees, giant leaves for publication,
(beatings from their branches is not in content or text).
Christmas star, christmas tree, mistletoe and holly
(but mother under everything in festival paralysis).
Old linoleum
                (she laid on that also
only it was daddy who kept her there those times).
My sister (but she cries at night).
My mates, play and otherwise
Yes I can sing of tornado nights on fire with
black passion and no dawn,
mouths that bleed from kissing.
Oh it was love love love
on our bathroom bedroom living room walls
(but that house fall and go boom in the 39 winds).

It seems there's nothing to sing out
this boyhood window
                        except her
                        across the street in the blue bushes,
                        my lady of the gold cloak
                        stringing silver bow and arrows,
                        wanting eyes
                        waiting for me as for no other.

Mother at your feet is kneeling
One who loves you is your child
Mother your altar boy is singing
In sob syllables of sugar breath
Mother cross my hands and hope to
                Death
Appropriate me from the living.

[1961]

34

Untitled

My sister has saved her body for years
knees hard on prayers
her elbows shrivelled from cold pillows.

And you, you have let her lie
in man-pride, she has not asked
only in prayers, Christ, a skinny voice
you have left her lying
soft in her pillow litanies to crucified arms.

Take me like breakfast take my hard prize
bring me on the river
to the hands of lovers

who give hard gifts away
all all of it
toss it over the Charles
go away on lights out to sea
be mingled in the current of a complete act.

Get off that hill bring good nails
let her know her blood freed
of our city
where only skin is passed out on the street.

[1961]

Bet'

If love be dark, a confusion in the mind
Then let me go, compelled and blind
Over the highway to your place where
Love is kind.

[c. 1961]

Ancient blue star!

seen out the car
window.
One blinking light
how many miles away
stirs in mind
a human condition

When paved alone
created of lust
we wrestle with stone
for answer to dust.

[c. 1962]

Where Fled

Despair long given me
as others' daily bread. What wish past this?
of wry stuff fed. Does desperate birth
bring one re-incarnation?

Night nurtures
trust in dawn. Let one scrap of light
disappear from afternoon, all
murmur: too soon/shadowed darkness falls.

Does doom come on? We continue
walking on. What walls. Fled by whom.
The moon's an easy answer
to shine through blood and clouds.

[1963]

You Do Not Come

I am nervous tonight. Your absence is a
strain. I turn and toss on the bed.
There seems some comfort in being dead.

a thought I could not have had
a few years ago, yet junk and tears
take their toll. The friends in jail

all make the world a different place
which could be redeemed by one look from love
on your unspeakable face.

now far removed,
now forever taken away.

[4.4.63]

Sickness

I know now I heard you speak in the night.
Voices of dead loves past,

whisper instructions over the electric air.
O words that confirm and chain.

Down deep the path's final entrance reveals itself.
The will draws strong on the palm of the hand.

Do not tamper with the message there.

[1963]

Prose Poem

The soul clings with its tenacity to the broken edge of life:

For a short moment we sit in the park opposite Washington Square Village. We are alone except for a group of Italian folk singers under the park lights old songs from *La Dolce Vita*.

We are not alone in our glamour, as we pass the pipe of Mariweedje between us, dreaming of Mexico and small Italian towns along the Mediterranean coast.

We exist upon the fringe of the world, small bright fragments that somehow burn away the fire's edge. We do not smoke. We scorch, but go on, bearing the scars.

So that others remark seeing us: Oh! how close they've been. And pass on, seeking the true flame's centre, working their way into oblivion.

[1963]

Night Samba

My mother sleeps in her bed,
a figure of the forgotten past

Priests asleep in Chestnut Hill
dream of lascivious young infantas.

Their dreams a shattered
Grenoble landscape.

When will I ever cross your mists,
saffron in the dawn?

Clouds hang over the mountain
It's such a long way
to attain the joys of yesterday.

Gone wild living begets mere sorrow.
When will I ever catch up with

that saxophone, Stan
Getz, you pestilence.

[1963]

Joy

burst in on us: a rare blossom.
Joie; a french word for happiness
that's just a thing called Joe.

Do you know him? He lives across
the border in provinces of grass.

Promise you tell him
I asked for him; you take me

To see him someday; a perfume
with his name on it

can be bought at Patou
for 12.50 ⅛ of an ounce.

It comes in
a green leather case
with gold cap, stitched up one side

his name
hollow letters of gold.

[1963]

Monday Sunrise

Red glow over China,
a color advertising
unable to duplicate

king's crown
burnished in chambers of North

seen over chimneys
on East River,

orange, yellow, tangerine

casts a mottled sheen
as of colour Renaissance, no
more Byzantine

Liquid
copper, bronze
topaz

    A scow sails into it,
      transformed from coal black
to Phoenician fishing boat
or submarine
raised in Yangtze

      shadows from the sea

turns a gown of
brocade or damask, a bracelet or heavy cross
of burning flame laid down upon the blue

its seething effervescence
become a poniard

stretching across banks
from Jersey to New York.

Not to mention the white
circle become a miracle upon it

                                        as Renoir knew
this gold, I think in hair
of yellow girls.

[c. 1963]

Jive

Tomorrow some motel with a guy,
Who'd have thought my dreams would come to this?
It's better than junk.
At least in a clean bed.

Then movies with mother.
The cycle goes on.
It's two o'clock in the morning
Rain on street.

After all, this toughness only goes to state
I'm out for anything
And will settle for nothing less. A dollar bill
Blows in the wind.

[1964]

"I despair of love . . ."

I despair of love
   ever throwing up
     on these shores,
enough of a raft for me
   to ride upon
     out to sea.

[1964]

On the Photograph of William Carlos Williams
Appearing as the Cover on the *Beloit Poetry Journal*

Oh my prince, my heaven
with flowers growing out of your head,
fingers pointing to the word,
sunflowers behind each ear.

does death never matter to others; o the men!
your space enclosed between these glasses,
your flesh hid beneath the grasses.
Bite the lip; it crumbles into dust.

Your words have not been heard.
The dirge remains unplayed.
Underground lie the beautys of men,
                              to their praise.

[1964]

Hypnagogic

By banks of the Neponset River
lies our house.
At night I hear voices of Indian spirits
call out to me:
'Each year these waters claim a pale face.'

I remember as children
how we built a hut to sit inside
hands touching in the dark,
how we sailed downstream on a raft
until Mother came through the woods
with a switch.
I remember an old well covered up with boards
and leaves, brown
from fallen trees,
birch and oak.

Winter now
boys skate on thin ice
by railroad tracks
they built a fence
no more will we see
that old woman, redhead
who floated downstream
bloated from the current,
nor She coming through the woods
curses on her mouth, in a red coat,
making her way to us
who sail on foamy rapids.

[1964]

Steve Magellanstraits

Black magician of the night
dive into the secrets of the sea
and come up with some golden fish
to perch on our mantels
through these long winter months
so that we may know
the currents of the inky storm
to come.

[Winter Solstice, 1964]

To Denise Levertov

1.

Is it really you come to me
      after all these years
  writing in darkness,
        only moon for light,
          head on my arms,
        hearing your feathers
      rustle   in flight
        these pages

2.

I hear you speak in the night
voice across miles.
Shall I turn on the light
to destroy this moment?

Tones of your voice fill shadows in that darkness
myself at your fountain,
beside me in the room.
Believe me, when I say it's enough.

No other in this world but you.
No therefore, or thereafter.
Your voice falls silent, when I listen,
When I pick up a pen to write, gone completely.

[1964]

50

Time

June, then September—life dredges past
as an avalanche. A week goes by
in the wink of an eye.
                              Friendships fall hollow,
old ghosts remain, carefully tendered
by the rain.
                    Streets of the cities, I have walked
                    My feet ache from the
miles, and yet they seem
a scant pathway to your door; where I sit
                                        now
contemplating old dreams that never change.

Old longings never subside; they rise in the breast
as tides of change that never rest.

This is the only eternity: what exists in the word.

[1965]

December 30

1AM

Sitting up by candlelight
Waiting for the right
voice to fall across inner ear
exact image to descend
and proper object to appear

out of a stream
rocks rise or reside
in middle of dream
opium shadow curtains hang
off eyelids, lips parched

(starch on mouth)
                    marched in
a line, refined the mind
to order's design,
eyes blind to glass swung
from stars one stung by the shine.

[1965]

An Evocation to Tommy Dorsey

sound of sycamores,
evening summer breeze,

telegraph cables zoom down the highway
Moonlight in Vermont.

The poem seizes one, in an experience
almost, all-consuming
as an orgasm

2.

It still blinds the eye,
sends electric waves through the ears,
causes blood to rise
to the top of the head.

Somehow makes my heart ache,
with all the frustrated desire of a lover.
Disappointment burns
like an empty light at the window.

That looks out, not on the street
but to a blank wall.   Blind
in the world we search for meaning
as most men bread.

3.
Kay Starr says this

perfectly, in her song,
So Tired.   "Tell me that
your thoughts are all of me, sweetheart."

4.
  I hymn the fates
                  that try to explain us.

in golden trousers,
doing Arabesques.

with candles of flame in each hand.

and soft blows upon our mouths.

The cardboard figures of dream
reside on the window-shelf.

At night, they lean out

to bend us to another dream,
than our own

Where agony, also is real.

[April 5, 1965]

No gods, mother, boys, beauty

It's too easy, begs description.
Defies the gods. Leaves something out
We were listening to other voices
in the afternoon: children, birds, ghosts
of haunted silence. Trucks.

Bells play across Columbus Avenue
I don't know why. We were asleep
In our pain. Another order descended,

where transmitted to an enchanted plain
behind intellect there was reason
and we were not commanded by gods, too.

[1965]

To Charles Olson

Who are these beasts
    staring out at the car window?
In your bedroom, in your barroom.
Do not let my stomach hang out
    do not let me become one of them.
The morning shines in on me.

[1965]

Fortitude

When I opened the window
I heard a bird sing
reassuring me every thing
would be all right.

My mother would get well.
There would be no harm from the dark
or intruders,
                    I would rise in the morning.

The sounds in the night
were friendly knocks—
and faces I saw at the door,
popping corks in the woods—

Were only ice breaking up,
my father was here
and springs in the bed
the only thing I had to be afraid of.

Now that I have written this
I but welcome sleep's kiss.

[1965]

Weir

Scollay Square
should've stayed
there with Dillinger
's harlots and squares.

All-night Rialto Theatre
no cloister neither
was Jack's tattoo parlor
or The Crawford House Bar.

Casino Burlesque; rubber-tired
that after hrs. joint on Hanover
Street, leading to Haymarket-Lechmere
No. Station trains bound for Gloucester,

Jack Hammond's Castle & Fort Square.

Without direction outré architecture
repairs slums of dereliction, or were
they, huddled in doorways at dawn, loving one another by milk, bottles, papers

at the Red Top Inn, Hayes Bick diner?
What confusion and violence stare here
in Buffalo, a solemn peace appeared divine
there those mannered streets of despair.

[1965]

Memories of You

Blown the fags in Central Park,
one after another, after midnight
in the snow; on park benches—
under the Japanese Pavilion.

Chased out of Bryant Park,
from behind the monument,
by a cop, with a big black buck.
I fingered his wedding ring
as I blew him. Fled to Boston

and the Esplanade where I was fucked
on the overpass by a student
while hundreds of cars raced by
below, unknowing of our ecstasy?

Returned to Bowery, where I found no one
except one man's hardon
in a doorway, facing the street

Thought of San Francisco, and Union Square,
nothing there and the park on top of Nob Hill,
where I cruised all dawn until finally
a man came out and took me up the backstairs
of the Bachelor's Club and blew me in the bathroom,
I think, locked. In my self? and what use

of this, this purgation of senses. Back to Boston,
jerking off on trains, I gotta stop taking
that wheat germ oil; find a negro at poetry reading
and he fuck me in "skyscraper" over Third Avenue.

Back to trees of Boston and Public Garden,
where I blew men all night long.
The stain is still on my face. How can I
face my brother, who first seduced me—
and my other brother, who I seduced—
and my mother and sister who prays for us all.

Now to Buffalo, where I do nothing—
but jerk off and think of Charles.
Bob Wilson blowing 78 men one weekend
on Fire Island where they serve an Olson martini.

Now back to New York and The Turkish Baths
which I find no fun, tho Frank O'Hara does,
and Allen Ginsberg sits in his white pajamas
and dreams of men as I do—and thinks of fame
at least used to but doesn't have to anymore,
as he is it. And I see what style this has degenerated into,
a vain pulling of my own prick and those of others.
When it was supposed to be a verbal blowjob of a poem.
And I have known women, too, laid beside them in the dawn—
but never balled them. Tho I want to.

Would some woman come up and give me enough of her flesh
so I could ball her and pretend she was a man,
For how else could I do it? For I have a woman's
mind in a man's body, and it would be lesbianism
otherwise, and it is a curse.

Unless some woman see and relieve me of this misery.

2.

For I will go to Spoleto and blow them there,
travel back to San Francisco and blow them there,
"get fucked in the ass by saintly motorcyclists"
would it were so; cruise Boston streets again
with Billy Donahue, pretend it is all peaches and cream
while inwardly I scream and dream of the day
when I will be free
to marry
and breed more children
so I can seduce them
and they be seduced by
saintly motorcyclists in the dawn.

[1965]

What Happened?

Better than a closet martinet.
Better than a locket
in a lozenge.
At the market, try and top it
in the Ritz.

Better than a marmoset
at the Grossets,
better than a mussel
in your pockets.
Better than a faucet
for your locker,
better not
clock it.
Better than a sachet
in your cloche,
better than a hatchet
in Massachusetts,
Ponkapog.
Pudget
Sound
lost and found.

Better than an aspirin—
aperitif does it.
Better not ask
how you caught it
what has happened to me?

Better not lack it—
or packet in at the Rickenbackers.
Better tack it back
in a basket
for Davy Crockett

Better not stack it.
Better stash it
on the moon.

Oh Pomagranate
ah Pawtucket.

Oh Winsocki or
Narragansett.

Better not claque it. Better cash it in
at Hackensack.
Better not lock it
up again.

[1965]

Dope

I am old no longer; youth is returned to me
after two sniffs of heroin: The Lift as Charles would call it; "have a whiff on me," they
said the old song went in California, as we crossed
the Golden Gate, with Joanne and Nem, Annie

Hatch, etc. Our faces show the strain
at 30. Hah, 30! we'll never see again
why heroin redeems us.

But I dont advise it to the young, or for
anyone but me. My eyes are blue.
                    Are yours too?

                    The rain falls
                    but not on me.

My skin gets a new lift, I dont need no food.
How long will this go on? Only till tomorrow

when I will collapse in a heap on the bed of the world.
Oh destiny, spare me!

Gold-blue jewels of the day. Opalescent rubies
of the moon. Amethyst of the sun. White marbles
at noon,   when the rain falls out
To our ankles. Grey tourmaline, Topaz from Mexico
brought back as booty, a golf ball to adorn
your little finger, can you lift your hand now to fuck the sun?

That's enough. I gotta lie down
                              with memories
                    as my only pillow,
        and rain drops the only thing
                    that's happening,
I wonder what the scene's like in New York.

Baby, I bet it's swinging. In the noon-day, sun.

[1965]

62

Ezra Pound at the Spoleto Festival 1965

His eyes were like stone. They pierced me from a distance. I felt I was in the presence of a god and afraid to look. We read first, and he followed from a box at the back of the theatre. His poems seemed direct complement to earlier ones read and to the relationship I had with Charles Olson, on our trip over from America:

> "It is not that there are no other men
> But we like this fellow the best,
> But however we long to speak
> He can not know of our sorrow."
>
> *T'ao Yua'n Ming*

He read other translations from the Chinese and Provençal, preceded by Marianne Moore's translation of La Fontaine's "The Ant and the Grasshopper." This first brought to my attention the fact that he was reading poems in direct relation to those gone before, although he knew nothing of them.

> "Pull down thy vanity, man
> the old man told us
> under
> the tent, you are over-
> run
> with ants."
>
> from *The Hotel Wentley Poems*

He read Robert Lowell's translation of the XVth Canto from Dante's Inferno, although I find no fact of its having been printed yet. The next afternoon, he read his own poems in the Piazza, but with the crowd pushing in, and Radio Nazionale Televizione, I could not hear more than Canto I. Fifteen minutes later, he was alone, with Olga Rudge, the widow Casells, myself and a village belle as companions. We sat together as the Spoleto sun set, in so blue a sky it can be seen nowhere else in the world.

It seemed strange, that the world, which had flocked to him earlier, now left him alone, and looked idly on across the square. So mildly he had signed their autographs, while cameras clicked. He did not mind, but had said to Desmond O'Grady earlier, "It's all wrong, they don't want me here, this is your generation, they don't want me here." The uniformed police, who had been in the audience the day before, to protect him from a Communist demonstration, had gone.

I sat back, far as I could, not to distract his eye, while he picked

63

calcium off his hands, with great determination. The reading began at five, now it was seven. I felt I was in the presence of a Chinese sage or mandarin. His hair was of the finest silk spun, a cocoon I thought, and when he rose to go, uttering no words one can hear, I thought, "He goes into the door of life, not death." I took his coffee cup and saucer off the table, into the cafe, and when I came out, I saw him for the last time, push open the brown door to Menotti's Villa.

Miss Rudge seemed a constant companion, and the evening before, we had gone to the theatre with him and Charles, Desmond O'Grady and his wife, after reading, with drinks in our hand, through the Piazza del Duomo. We saw Leroi Jones' *Dutchman*, and asking him after, what he thought of the play, Pound said, "Tremendous," to Charles going up the stairs. "Holy Ireland, alive in O'Grady" he wrote on a postcard to a friend of O'Grady's back in Ireland. We sat in the front row. Charles broke his glass.

We walked through the theatre lobby, the three of us abreast, by the palm trees, around a corner, in military formation.

Charles read the next day, after Caresse Crosby arrived. Afterwards, she told us at her villa outside Rome, Rocca Sinibalda, that Pound had visited her a few days previous, and read the poems of Harry Crosby to her in the garden. He had written the notes for the original edition of *Torchbearer*, when it appeared in The Black Sun Press, 1931.

While we were sitting in the Piazza that last day, a young man approached us, and asked if he might show Pound a photograph of a Renaissance prince he had found in the library. Pound said yes, and the man pulled from his portfolio a lovely portrait whose name I do not know, but Pound glared thoroughly, and knew. It was himself. The man thanked the Maestro and left.

[1965]

Ally

My father's black ashtray
hollowed out of 1930 foes
of woe and death

he let me have at home, on
choking highways of disease through
Canton Avenue, Brush Hill Road

Blue Hills Parkway. Bought anew
in 1932? it stands here still
to fill the sad stuffed cigarettes

of Philip Morris, Ltd.

[1966]

The Rose at the End of the Saloon

I saw flowers when I thought of you—
golden flowers on a hill.
That's enough for me.

I don't like those words.
Last testament to a song.

A bunch of old photographs
I handed to my mother,
                          weeping on the couch.

[1966]

For Huncke

Know no other god than this:
the man who places on your mouth
a kiss. Keep no mystery
but his who whispers memory.

Though he lead you to the desert
or over hills where famine
flowers, like the locust
he devours what he loves most.

Saving none for tomorrow, or dawn
comes with empty arms, and he knows no way
to feed himself, feeding off others,
he has many, who find him, help him

you be one and dedicate your life
and misery to the upkeep of this cheapskate
you love so much no one else
seems to bridge the gap

with their common habits and rude manners,
his never were, a perfect gentleman
who leaves no trace, but lingers through the room
after he has gone, so I would follow

anywhere, over desert or mountain,
it's all the same if he's by my side.
The guide and wizard I would worship and obey,
my guardian teacher, who knows how to stay

alive on practically nothing in the city
until help comes, usually from a stranger or youth.
Such I am or was who knew no better
but all that I better forget now since I met you

and fell into that pit of the past with no escape.
You knock on the door, and off I go with you
into the night with not even a cent in my pockets,
without caring where or when I get back

But if once you put your hand on my shoulders
as David Rattay did last evening
that would be enough, on the seventh night
of the seventh moon, when Herd Boy

meets the Weaving Lady in heaven
and wanders forever lost in arms
until dawn when you come no more.

[1966]

"Some black man looms in my life . . ."

Some black man looms in my life, larger than life.
Some white man hovers there too, but I am through with him.
Some wild man dreams through my day, smelling of heroin.
Some dead man dies in my arms every night.

[1966]

Parking Lot

Don't give nothing for nothing,
yet I blew a guy today
for eight dollars.

He gave me nothing.
I paid him.
O sin that wreaks vengeance

on them lidden children of the world.
I stole the money from Steve Jonas,
'bread from a poet.'

Damned and cursed before all the world
That is what I want to be.

[1966]

Grown Out of Habit

Benzedrine diners
open after midnight
took another chance
things would work out right.

Madness, illness or detour,
who could know, who would care?

before our body went like a light
our mind wasted, restored through

rain glistened places
outside our window

                a blue candle
                in poems by Andrew Lang.

A surprised heron, night
to delicate fabrics
sang   did not care,

We simply arrived
there and found illumination beyond
repair in all night diners
going nowhere.

[1966]

To H.

I like Sunday evenings after you're here.
I use your perfume to pretend you're near
in the night. My eyes are bright, why
can't I have a man of my own?

Your wife's necklace's around my neck
and even though I do shave I pretend
I'm a woman for you
you make love to me like a man.

Even though I hear you say why man
he doesn't even have any teeth
when I take out my plate
I make it up to you in other ways.

I will write this poem.

[1966]

Berkeley St Bridge

Petrified the wood
wherein we walk.

Frozen the fields.

Cruising these empty city streets
gets you nowhere.

Will you ever be saved, John?
I doubt it.

This world's got nothing for me.

[1966]

Waste

Poetry a noble art, it
comes from well born sons.
Futile for me to start
As to see a midnight sun.

What landscape of the heart
May I set pattern to?
Arteries, pulmonary chart
Or where veins run blue?

I know the vessels' cart
Stained gold, black velvet hung
But of its richer part
Know none.

[c. 1967]

To D.

Forgotten what I once loved
a good haircut and a manicure
early death, the loneliness

of summer afternoons on apple boughs;
down the brook up the field.

Before the parch of adolescent love,
dirty boys together by the stream
surprised caretakers in what they do

climbing over dams behind
blind pebbles lane

Under bushes my first come,
first served forgetting the world
renascence at their feet

yearning to be caught, held
in crushes' obedient trust.

[1967]

74

Paul

It's nice under your hands
a stranger whom I've never met
before tonight but twice

It's nice beside you on the bed
where my heart bled for love.
It's nice to have you here

and having said that, dear
nice to feel your hands upon my hair
and nicer still, to know we will

meet again, start off where
your girl friend, mistress, what ever

she is, that sleeping bride
will not be on your other side.

[1967]

1930 Jazz

rocked me in my cradle, While Papa was in
the madhouse, Mama
on welfare,
Billie was at the Savoy with Count
Basie singin' Swing it, Brother
Swing and I kicked my bootied feet
in time to Teddy Wilson.
Papa, walk Tremont Street again
in the fog, let your bald head shine
like a full moon
between bars.

Stop this diddle daddle.

There is time for nonsense, romance
and forgetting.
Deep rhythm stimulates me, hot
rhythm captivates me,
to the next fix,

New York, Boston, San Francisco.
The scene widens as the years
we walk with a cane. Dont stop
to diddle daddle, stop
this foolish prattle.
Come on, swing me Count.
Swing it, brother swing.

[1967]

Memories of Gerrit

The maiden's prayer haunts this afternoon, without you, the day is
    bleak, dull
without you, my dear; still the night holds unexpected promises

Champagne in the evening, golden dawns, cab rides through streets
of rain, afternoons on avenues in Cambridge,
Orchestra seats and German jazz, lonely vigils over the sea, yachts;
Florida and Maine, the geography of your soul, transporting dirty
    pictures
through Times Square; sado-masochism in the upper echelons of
    Manhattan.

The Maiden's Prayer haunts the castle, as white wine, washes over
    Norman's Woe.
Magic played on the keyboard, heard in Cairo and learned by rote
from the Master Therion in 1908.

Sax Fifth Avenue clothes but that was another man

[1967]

Preface

Verse making is more than a continuum of principle resting on feminine phenomenological apprehension. The real one of many, the illusory far and near intersect to push behaviour's stream, dependent on questing, producing revelatory postures for men, animals and stars.

The poet is one pastor of this distribution between two visions.

Illusory form heightened by denial arises from contraction of desire, stilling propagation. To stay with one's self requires position and perhaps provision, realizing quality out of strangeness.

The quality of gift being alone.

Wraiths cross time.

The gift of quality seems rather removed from processes practiced today over the counter, behind the bar and desk in lobbies of service. Interferences from gifts hamper realization, but they may be used as reinforcement of sensory apparatus. Proximate distractions show little more than confusion and to promulgate them as verse scatters ultimate sights, the true brothered quality of what we condense and what to allow constant.

The permanent evident search for labour and trial makes dignity trivial. Visual order obeys gravity, but genuine shimmering substance cognates more than complacencies of constant worth. It holds radiation, that force attracts, draws and breathes.

An indoctrination to quality could be a return to places of origin, one instance of namely objects, the second an absolute rendition of balance and movement, the third transformations by fire, the easiest of all, if will be inherited. To true the present gleams more than conditions of pseudo-morphology, it asks one to submit to discipline's enduring form.

[1968]

78

Solitaire

Never stole nothing
of women's thoughts

eight twists, four loops
five circles one confinement

make a sentence.

never stole drugs
or a packet of books

never stole truth
or water, only flesh:

controlled nerves, come-
ly bones, clean

pedestal for clumsy
spin:
      results in

dependence to rear,

see what the half-blind
desire of men declare,

rather than die alone
in an empty chair,

whispering to evening
air kinder than girl's

residence.

[1968]

Chop-House Memories

We took a boat to Provincetown one spring day, just Frank O'Hara and myself, to visit Edwin Denby, the poet, who lived all summer on the dunes, while Frank was in Cambridge at the Poets' Theatre on a Rockefeller Foundation grant. We worked together on John Ashbery's *The Compromise* or *Queen of the Caribou*; and on plays of Hugh Amory and V. R. Lang, not to mention Mary Manning's adaptation of *Finnegans Wake*.

Frank introduced me to various poets before this, Edwin Muir, James Merrill, George Montgomery, May Sarton, and John La Touche and had sublet for that winter and spring of 1956 Lyon Phelps' apartment on Massachusetts Avenue, where we two met to read poetry once. He wanted me to visit Mr. Denby, who had been dance critic for the *New York Herald Tribune* during the early forties and who also wrote verse.

Frank worked on *Art News* sporadically as a critic and during the cruise to Provincetown, suggested I move to New York and write for them.

The hard, wooden planks of seats below deck, choppy waves as we sailed through Boston Harbor, sordid memories of lost love's jazz morning's intermingled in our devotion to each other so forced to change our mind often we roamed listlessly above deck fore and aft in search of surcease from the throbbing motors of the boat.

We both thought of suicide as the final resolution of our desire as we stood again below deck by the hectic Atlantic cutting at our feet, speaking of Hart Crane and the last words we would have in our mouths at that moment of surrender. Only chains saved us from its vengeful force. Masses of seagulls followed us down the coast and dark clouds forbade our entry into Provincetown Harbor.

Seated on the side of the dance floor we waited, music drifted out of the bar and told of the inability to dock on Cape Cod because of inclement weather. We glumly returned to Boston and my room on Hancock Street.

We had met Jack Spicer previously at the Harvard Gardens, and while I read my poetry in the humid summer evening of Beacon Hill, the both of them wept through the incipient rain and electric-charged air.

It was a dreadful room infested with roaches, as I mention in my Scenario for a Film published with Selected Poems, over twelve years later.

At that time Frank was always asking me for poems and when the Poets' Theatre took *Finnegans Wake* to New York for production at the YMHA Poetry Center, I went along and visited his rooms 90 University Place, which he shared with Joseph LeSueur, who worked for a while then at the Holliday Bookshop, and he got one printed in John Bernard Myers' *Semi-Colon*, out of the Tibor De Nagy Gallery on West 57th Street, writing me before that for them; the one called "With Mr. J R Morton" was my first published poem outside of undergraduate work.

We corresponded before that while I was a student at Black Mountain College in North Carolina and he says, July 21st, 1956:

How are things down there in the South, where men are men and girls are glad? Are you writing lots and what is it like? Here it is raining and sort of light-grease-colored. It's been fairly cool and I've been out to visit Larry a couple of times and gone swimming etc., but haven't gotten up to New Hampshire yet. I think I may go before August and work is upon me, but inertia prevails and I just read all the time. Can't write. I took your tip on Lawrence and read Aaron's Rod and am now in Kangaroo. Yes, he is marvellous. I used to have a lot of his poems but I can't find them now in this pig-sty and am dying to read The Ship of Death and get cheered up.

I met Jimmy Schuyler while out at Larry's, since he's staying in Southampton for the summer and he seemed very well and asked for you. He's at c/o Fairfield Porter, 49 South Main St., Southampton, NY, if you want to write him. I remember you said you wanted to, did you?

John Button and I saw one of the all time great movies the other day, LA STRADA and man, was it ever! It has Anthony Quinn, Richard Basehart (what a nice last name) and someone named Giulietta Masina who is a genius, she's the End. Also the director, Federico Fellini seems to have a few insights into the soul not often granted by the Heavenly Hiders. Do you know this poem of Thomas Hardy?!

"Had you wept; had you but neared me with a
hazed uncertain way,
Dewy as the face of the dawn, in your large and
luminous eye,
Then would have come back all the joys, the tidings
had slain that day,

And a new beginning, a fair fresh heaven, have
*   smoothed the things awry.*

But you were less feebly human, and no passionate
*   need for clinging*
Possessed your soul to overthrow reserve when I
*   came near;*
Ay, though you suffer as much as I from storms
*   the hours are bringing*
Upon your heart and mine, I never see you shed a tear.

The deep strong woman is weakest, the weak one is the
*   strong;*
The weapon of all weapons best for winning, you have
*   not used;*
Have you never been able, or would you not, through
*   the evil times and long?*
Has not the gift been given you, or such a gift you refused?

When I bade me not absolve you on that evening or
*   the morrow,*
Why did you not make war with me with those who weep
*   like rain?*
You felt too much, so gained no balm for all your torrid
*   sorrow,*
And hence our deep division, and our dark undying pain."

I went to his reading later that year at the Poetry Center after my return from Black Mountain and heard for the first time publicly his sonorous notes on the film industry in crisis and his Elegy to James Dean, whose photograph, now in my possession, he had stuck to the wall of Lyon's apartment, and his memorable "Ode on George Washington Crossing the Delaware." Allen Ginsberg and Peter Orlovsky met us after at a small German restaurant on Lexington Avenue and we cabbed downtown together for the first time to the *old* Five Spot in Cooper Square. Allen was unknown then and sat on my lap and Frank accused me of liking him too much.

We were both at the terminus of separate love affairs and would console each other on the banks of the Charles, the old Cronins' off Howard Square and upstairs at Joe's over Wursthaus for the mistakes we made, one loving too desperately and the other

too hard. How mad we were on moonlit nights and railway stations, bidding farewell and future encounter.

Meet again we did, at Morris Golde's apartment for an evening soirée, with Aaron Copland in attendance, Virgil Thomson,
Marc Blitzstein and Alvin Novak, at his own apartment, where
I was a house-guest to meet John and Jane (Wilson) Gruen and take
phone messages from Grace Hartigan and Jane Freilicher, and at
his close friend's John Button, finally to meet Edwin Denby, whose
calligram by Frank I later was to see in print.

Our friendship lapsed when I moved to California in October
of 1957, though I did get to see all of *Second Avenue* years before
it appeared.

His earlier work had been brought to my attention also and
I remember what delight *A City Winter and Other Poems* elicited,
before he was surrounded by museum vagaries and lesser-known
versifiers. What pleasure to meet years later when he was truly
well-known, and living off Tompkins Park. I would visit him in
the half-dark apartment before poetry readings and off to dinner
at Sing Wu with Kenneth Koch and Kynaston McShine, whose
friendship Frank and I shared, then later on Broadway for a small-
time Saturday afternoon and the crowded events of John Ashbery's
return from Paris and Edwin's 60th birthday party, upstairs, with
Stella Adler, Rudolph Burckhardt, LeRoi Jones, Bill Berkson and
Barbara Guest as faithful guests.

News of his death was a painful shock. I had written him from
Italy the summer before of the great joy the poetry festival he had
arranged for us with Gian-Carlo Menotti brought and how I longed
for him to be north of Rome, with Stephen Spender, Charles Olson
and Ezra Pound.

Little did we know those summer weekends would be so
disastrous and that the simple fun of Fire Island or Race Point
would run out such a pointless end. Poignant hoydens, we reviled
death, as witness his words on V. R. Lang:

> "Well it's just as well that we didn't write each other sooner
> since I've been fiendishly depressed. Isn't Bunny's thing the
> worst thing that ever happened, I mean in my life (because
> with love ruined you can always see your way to blaming
> yourself for a few things and then give yourself some post-
> mortem whacks or I do anyway), but I never really thought
> such a thing could happen. But I have gotten out of it
> somewhat, not meaningfully, I don't know how, but am in

it less frequently, so it just nags and makes me feel tiresome and malevolent and malicious and not feeling like doing the world no good. Or life or god. Fuck that. It is a hopeless dealing because if I did reach a rationale it would mean I had adjusted, it would mean nothing to her being, and what we want to do is alter if not destroy facts, isn't it? I mean is it? I'm sorry, this is fruitless."

[May 1968]

Loss

To live without the one you love
an empty dream never known
true happiness except as such youth

watching snow at window
listening to old music through morning.
Riding down that deserted street

  by evening in a lonely cab
    past a blighted theatre
oh god yes, I missed the chance of my life

    when I gasped, when I got up and
      rushed out the room
        away from you.

[1968]

Permanent

All beauty dies, past
especially the love
in love with loveliness
and youth, how vain,

how bittersweet, this might
be the last night we need
meet, quick the pace,
rapid the feet, as

the tune persists in the
ever constant moon,
its reason clear by contrast.

[1969]

May

There are certain poems I wrote
that never can be set down
Or remembered note by note.

For I wrote them in my mind,
before I laid them on paper.
These are the perfect poems of the birds,
Eagle and hawk, the sparrows Philip,
at noon tell of tomorrow.

The perfect poems of war, lad to lad,
That I composed only in my mind,
and never on paper may be had.

[8.17.69]

The Take for Granteds

Past Duchamp as though his mother were sainted
as though his sister continues prophecies against politicians' wives,
in Rosanno Schiaffano's mind, actually a black tiger against
rags of reportage. Emilia, I died for you, it's true,
a face honest, brave and courageous,
that may take a bullet wound,
hacked by outrageous sound from
indigenous wounds off ancient coins.

Thelma Mary Patricia Ryan

[January 6, 1970]

Doggerel

Alone in an afternoon's
misery, but not so compromised
as unable to compose, unable

to wander the fields, the lanes

the sunlight wanders on the
windowsill. The dial on the radio,
the man closing a car door, or

running water in the room next door.

No elation, only this effort
to combat nervous anxiety.
Some might call it heroic:

when I have memories of other afternoons
they do not last, nor shall this one.

[1970]

White Rum and Limes

Bulgarian lilies, trans
sylvanian tulips on a
rose quartz stair-case bend
beneath sunrise Hun-
garian roses twisted to shape

a balcony green iron before
the lawn in Madison, where Rita
Nolan fixes brunch for Friday's
flight to Washington, D.C.

the twelve hours of desire above cruise
through vacant chambers where
J. Foster Dulles sips a martini, anx-
ious to depart the blowing windbirds

talk of Farouk and Millia Gluck.

[July 4, 1970]

What I Imagine to Be My Love Whispers in the Corner

Those who stay at home
often worship far away places
and unattainable ambitions,

such as fame and idealized love.
Those who travel find their dreams come
true, meet fantastically interesting persons

through talent and achievement, even
of a minor sort. I have moved all

my adult life, finding success sweet
when I came home in overt defeat
forgot it and settled down to a routine,

to wake up at those out of the way places,
with hands full of familiar feelings,
a new sense of glamor pervaded the scene.

Oh yes, this is that bus station known at twenty years old,
and now past thirty-five, in good health, I sit
at the same tables, bearing the moon and its dream from the
    fifties

rushing down Charles Street, on fire with desire for
beautiful women, bubbling alcohol, late hours, smart cafes
fast limousines more demanding assignments on my energy.

             —John Wieners 1970 St. James Street Boston, 2 PM
                           Waiting for Gerard and Rene

Hotels

From the first dollar-a-night rooming house on Tremont Street to the Plaza may seem a long jump, from the Broadway Hotel in San Francisco to the Dorothy Statler Suite in Buffalo half a continent, from New England Inn on Cape Cod to an Indian hacienda in Santa Fe part of the great divide, through the Biltmore, the New Yorker, and One Fifth Avenue to one night stands in Canton, Ohio, rainy motels, cabins and motor inns across the United States, penniless in The Dixie in Times Square, the Thomas Jefferson only for scoring heroin, The Nassau, Blackstone, Chateau Frontenac in Quebec to creepy Bowery Broadway Central, the Gattapone, overlooking a 14th century aqueduct in mountains, north of Rome. The Atlantic with Charles Olson, near the Stazione Terminale, The Rockefeller Hilton, Parker House, Hotel Madison, all these acquired mystery for writing, the Hotel Victoria, George Washington, Chelsea, Ritz Hotel in Montreal, Hotel Albert, Earle, Marlton, The Rhinebeck Inn on The Hudson, oldest inn in America, The Hotel Ithaca since torn down outside Cornell, and the hotels this book will be a record of, after the YMCA in Washington, D.C. and Albergo Nationale of Rome, the Commodore in Cambridge with friends and in anonymity, a lover's manor on the North Shore, a forgotten accommodation in amnesia and a borrowed room at The Hotel Wentley for a beginning . . . not accounting for the Hotel Adelphi in Saratoga.

*

By this time I checked into the Delmonicos on Park Ave., the hashish was gone and I was left with marijuana, old friends gone.
You are up now and moving about the house.
I am going to a strange hotel, Manhattan
heart beating loudly. With a snake ring for
luck and pomade on my lips. Lapels too wide,
thinking of 1950, in the stink of Mayfair.

*

Hotels I have stayed in and NEVER robbed
not once, not even the thought of it, not skipped the bill
ever once, or left without Paying!

92

The Hotel St. Moritz,   1 Dollar a Night

The Hotel Statler, while coming up to Boston for The Ziegfeld
        Follies with the Champagne and Dinner in the Room $40

The Buffalo Statler-Hilton as a guest of Ms. A.S. Overnight No tab.
        Barely got out free with my freedom as The Hereditary
        Grand Duke, Jean of The Grand Ducal House of Luxem-
        bourg, 2 room Suite, no fare, as guest of Billy Hutton, from
        Grosse-Pointe, good luck, Billy I miss you. Love on the
        twin-beds as Claudia "Lady-Bird" Johnson spoke on the
        television Set. What a gas, as he ordered a table of 2
        whiskeys, full-food, and Ed Dorn and Jenny, Marianne
        Faithfull's cousin came to visit later, Bill looked so cute
        in his gaucho torniquet, and toreador sailor Levi pants.
        What a doll, Billy; I'll be seeing you. And speaking of dolls,
        that Ed Dorn is no small shakes as a knock-out, Himself.
        Doll, Ed, bless you. You keep the old Home Fires burning
        on my Monday A.M. Linen. The evening before of course,
        quiet in my Rooming House, Ed lent me and spent me on
        40.00. It's not the first time for him to stand me.

                                    *

The Hyatt-Hilton, as The Beverly Hills-Hilton was filled from a
        convention, 10th Floor, no food, no champagne,
        one night only. Gosh, James Mason loved it! I bare-
        ly got in as Zsa Zsa Gabor overnight, with my bags
        in the lobby next morning, that Joseph Magnin cost
        me 20 dollars, plus The Fiddlers past The Palms,
        and the maids, no tip,
how I miss them like
The Bismarck, in Chicago, where it seems the same room clerk that
directed around the corner from The Hyatt-Regency I believe, I may
be wrong drove me, after missing that 10 PM to Michigan's O'Hare;
gosh, how I dread missing my flite. He got me in there though and
I don't believe I paid until the next morning, although I know I did.
A great cantankerous remodeled plush accommodation right down the
street from The Bus Terminal, where I caught the Detroit-bound vehi-
cle for a nominal fee. Detroit looked so wonderful from The Howard
Johnson's Motor Lodge Windows, although I did not arrive by car. They
let me in too, after a full, good meal in the lobby, off the side street,

near the wonderful famed Pulaski Circle, winging its way onward to the so swingingly recalled Canadian Border, southerly The Beverly Wilshire looked wonderful, as I told you, off Stockton, California. Two nights there. They are so suchly rely prim and proper, I couldn't dare to take a cocktail in the boite, tho I promised myself one, instead entertained a Local Radio Station tycoon in my lovely, adorable, perfection's chalet king-size minus reservation. Oh, those Chinese are so wonderful. They keep a saint spirit up.

*

More Hostelries)

The Nassau, New York, recommended by Bobby Driscoll, no, wait a minute, rather the English Professor, and Poet, David Posner, Extraordinaire, he married the English Heiress Olivia Wedgwood. Germaine code. God bless her, she's around still, globe-hopping, tripping, travelling from one International port to the next, David said Nassau, and so I went. As Mrs. Dick Nixon. I had been there, and Bobby the genius came up with me, and rich socialite from Buffalo, his mother went to Vassar, and his Father's a Banker, and his sister's Diana, I think; and I wrote a poem for David, and he had beautiful hair, and the most amazing purblind complexion, he'll come back, David always will. And his sister and mother and Father, and their attic room, and solarium, and the mother's desk, with the Upper class girl's school College, rather bulletin. I think all three of us enjoyed ourselves enroute to Castalia in Millbrook. Dr. Timothy Leary's Foundation, New York.

*

University Manor, that was a place, where I met him, with Allen Ginsberg, and the then Rosemary Leary, before the German nuptials, how exciting, glamourous, speedy and up to the point, they read, and sound over the cool Albany evenings, they shall stand it, again, with memories of Onetta's; my first child, without birth; Bill's Luncheonette, and the 200 dollar Tab finally paid for; Rose, Kurt Fiedler, Leslie's son, the Doctore-Poet, who wrote all through the Forties, and Fifties, and Sixties, and now Seventies, his loving family, Kurt, Michael, and Eric; so many stayed at The University Manor, my mother among them, before we crossed Customs, to The General Brock, for an evening dinner, dancing, and listening to the Radiobroadcast high above the swirling North Country Avalanches. On The Maid of The Mist.

94

Sheraton-Plaza; Copley Square, one night, the hash, postage, about 40 dollars, but I was going out of my mind, with jitters up North, or East, or West, possibly over the Mississippi. As The Biltmore; the Chateau-Frontenac; The Albergo Nazionale; The Hotel Atlantico in Rome; The Gattapone; The Plaza when Mr. Olson was dying, unfortunately I did not pay; suspect in Akron, Ohio I may have, a double room with his legator, Harvey H. Brown, III, with the orchestra down below, and the violin strings plucking serenely against the impending news of his January 10th departure. Only 4 years ago, and 16 or so days, in little Manchester Cemetery on the west side of town.

I got into a few Inns in my life. R.I., N.Y., Amherst, mostly small apartments or quiet roadside drops losing mischief subtracted make-believe.

Princeton's Nassau Inn is a different story; sedate somewhat misty after my *Response*; then up around the Toll Roads shuttered for an English nephew to The British Communist Party. His name's John Temple. Good-hearted John, I still wear his dressing-gown, as I write, and Knit Kickers over the replastered entrances behind kilnfired Chambers.

⋏

My missing Hotel Registry List will soon turn up. There's been not enough returned because personal atrocization, so many stars, planets demoted over venial catastrophe. Or lienned insurance tenure violators. When your time's up, brother, you've had it, murder incorporated, or not. Death-knell vestry abyssmals from Roxbury or Jamaica Plain, Culver-Webb CC's calm BillerVickers Peckapickpalfreypotatoes. Conrad-Hueffeur's *The Inheritors*. P.T.

Let's see, compared to the money my mother spent on me, I maybe laid out 4 Bills on The FleaMarket. She threw away about 6000 of them to keep me over the 4 decade Beatrice Peel Hall, unh, not Albermarle, Loans and All, Stallionhurdle. Horses, bulls, and studs, that's my furlough from Fudgeque frycharisma. If you can find them out in your lobbies these days, and I did, as well as I do, Rhinebeck's Astorm Beekman Arms, and Saratoga Spring's *Adelphi*. Gosh, how the mane's ply. Where next, scootyPeregrin, floralwraith. Snootyaural. Sootyurals.

[1970]

What Happened in the Woods at Rockingham County

We loved under the tops of long grass
the sun of your ear in
                    my eyes
the wind pushed but not
                      between us
one
   in the sharp grass.

Calamus, he said.
The ants moved over you not
fast as my fingers
                wrote with weeds
a name on your back
whiter than the sun
                came down
                      with swallow
over tops of the grass
              we were in,
                  (love)
naked.

[1971]

Withered on the Stem

supplicant against the system
dead heat
between foe & aggression

it behooves little
if our civil war
removes oppression from your home

the Petty Lounge stands Saturday
upstairs rain
Ronnie the girl in my lady's room

plays with toilet paper by the roll
while she got on
the dumbo in your mind

to no avail stud.

[c. 1972]

Women

As a young prince of the United Kingdom, and as a president in the United States, my prior thought was to consider the general editorship of *Vogue* magazine in mind to addition my revered, though backward impression of woman, and especial women, who have pleased me, in public and, or in private.

*

First came to my memory Melissa Hayden, off-Broadway, smoking and having an excellent rehearsal break from the City Center Ballet. I felt graced in her presence and most respectful toward her enormity of language vernacular. She sensed vitally herself and the difficulties encountered through her genius, of towing the mark and remaining as a toast to the accolades of gentlemanly audiences. The holiness of technicality reinforces my thought that to mention the defects and limitations of others conditions assoluta supremacy.

*

A girl, as trained as herself, continues to amuse though dancing, or dunning the dispersion patently straining lesser rungs from concentrations, gone awry over frantic guilt, that must be admitted intensely of others. She had in 1963 an inspiring gaze, soothing mobilization and meticulous control of private gestures, grandiose pointing and powerful formentation to frame premeditation, necessary to assume intuitively imperative ambition.

*

Another dancer I completely worship is Madame Vera Lorina, that is Vera with a capital V, whom I met in Spoleto, in 1965, as John Wieners, the poet from Buffalo, invited along with Frank O'Hara and Gian-Carlo Menotti, to honor the arts of symphony and song, including sibillance on the East Coast. Miss Lorina after my recitation inquired or stated she had seen my poems or verses or poetry in *Harper's Bazaar*. What an honor!

*

I replied that Kenneth Rexroth had mentioned my name in his article on writers in Harper's Magazine, that year, but she had not mistaken one for the other. I was so disappointed that the verses that I had denied at the time, earlier were written as Edna St. Vincent Millay. Genre *de femme* maintains excellence in contemplating the gorgeous Vera Lorina, a Norsewoman I had for twenty-five years adored as a star, in *I Married An Angel* ****.

*

She gave so unstintingly of herself, when we walked across the square, north of Rome, in the face of the photographers. Very little money was expended for the events of those few afternoons on the town, in the mellow sunlight of early July. We were all mentioned in the Italian Press.

*

Frank O'Hara could not attend. Even I had to borrow a $1000, still unpaid, to reach the Festival. Miss Lorina, in direct honesty, mentioned the fact that her husband was in Japan, at that present, and her marvellous excitement at introducing me to her choreographer, John Butler, kept her in mind afterwards.

*

I went out of my way, upon returning to school, to hear her recite the evocative words to *Persephone*, a concerto in four parts by Igor Stravinsky, a Russian maestro who has bowled over the younger, more naive audiences of this twentieth century. It was a joint collaboration.

*

The various aspects of women cause shimmering auras I would never arouse, from their odes, ballads and opus. For duenna, women is a strange term. Woman is even worse. Dangerous, when a young man attains their princeliness, pricelessness and precociousity.

*

Watching Leonardo da Vinci, I remember his gentleness, and know women possess this, fabulously. I actually encountered Michelangelo outside the Sistine Chapel visiting the Vatican, after meeting Madame Lorina, and thinking of my mother.

*

Writing Miss Lorina's name, I thought of her as a prima total ballerina, of course, without question, and she has retained her lithe figure, lissome coiffure and marvellous charms, above and beyond any teen-school model, including ingenuity.

*

Working without guidelines here, I abjectly suspicion retrograde aspersions as to why I do not accept this Assignment as an insult; and capitulating I initiate my circumspection without either summation or interlocution, acquiring definition of women from professional certainty, and not bigamous facts.

*

I admire strong, determined girls, bringing to mind, one from a small town, where I was reared, known formerly of Miss Nancy Callaghan. Trusting, buoyant and superior to experiences on the surface, she has married well, as I did not think she would, and I am glad for she deserves it. Strong, thrifty and most agreeable to acquire practice.

*

Truth I do not expect from a working woman. Protection I do, both in offering and affording. That is what I do through these words.

*

I pray God will return Nancy Callaghan to my person. Mother loved her and pleased me in agreeing that she believed in the small, elaborate arts of docility, impeccability of apparel and loyal customedness.

*

—Two—

Limited in space, I will list other attributes of woman.

Beauty
Warmth
Holiness
Devotion
Food
Assent

*

Wealthy born, I aspire to Marlene Dietrich, Judy Garland, Garbo and Lana Turner, all multi-millionaires and male-oriented. Studying no habits of girls, youth, matrons and scholars, I conspire alone to return glamour and excitement out of the tedium, apparent in some monotonous tasks, they must undertake.

*

Singing, dancing, acting are not the only particularities I go out of my way for instruction.

*

Ingrid Bergman has that homeliness I once paid for, and savor. Awkward clumsy compatability as cognoted in our commerce. It does not as I witnessed on stage offer defeat. Nordic looks strengthen our expensive participation among leading ladies.

*

Endless the list is, that I portently garner. Perhaps to be born a princess is the best solution to a lady's commune. Skills of belle design and bastionship conduce fervor, hearkening comradely congress. Our senators, Margaret Chase Smith, and Congresswoman, Phyllis Webb, to name only two of a broad group I know exists scintillate the spoke of national leadership, stretching out of D.C. to B.C.

*

Queen Elizabeth another libertaterian I wholeheartedly espouse keeps supreme attributes.

Challenge

Knowledge

Wisdom   and in closing I announce Rose Kennedy and Jacqueline Onassis as tantamount heroines to survive the dinginess of ugly politicians, who drink and bawl at others' expenses.

*

Girls I have seen in passing to endear these words on woman are Babs Hutton and Patricia Dilde Shattuck.

*

Pronounciation, good jaws and strong legs maintain money. Countless decades, from publicity and dependability produce a manager as Catherine Huntington of Pinckney Street on Boston's Beacon Hill, to introduce us to courtly tradition and motivated culture. Without these terms, no species could exist. Defilements of baboon, or ravenous sparrows puncture the adjuncts to adulthood and alliances between man and woman.

*

I have never married and never shall, either as prince, or president allowing papacy. See to it that women are not affected by these choices towards anherence of insignia and insularity.

*

Delightedly, a novice conveyance upon unproven staples propositions permanent chariness.

*

24 Chestnut Circle
Hanover, Massachusetts
[Jaunary 8, 1972]

Grey Sabbath

after dropping $500 at the racetrack
    conversation builds rampant somehow in The Beacon
        Chambers restaurant
  Sunday afternoon this October. The cloudy overcast harbor
and morning coffee combine to combat our mid-day miasma at
                                  missing
  one another through far ports. New York, Frisco oceans beat
        down at our moorings,
    forcing new friendship, in place of those Fifty assumptions
    trembling before surrender to past hoydens. Oh loss
  or gain, what do you prefer? While you stumble on this planet
      planning new assaults
  before the void fresh days awake. Strangers appear
bearing masks of absent friends, an old man with blue eyes of my
      dead mother
sits before a window with geraniums, smoking eternal Luckys and
    nursing daily Buds.

[1972]

Yonnie

1

Beneath the ivory lady
  of mercy
Red wings
upon a silver tray
a gold bracelet laid
there before retiring.

Real love, at last
half-pretending, half Creel-
eys,
    her voice
            as if youth should go on forever
    beneath a blue star.

2

Listening in the dark
to a piano thirty years old,
it's not as in the old days,
when I got up,

    I had to cross the room
    to turn on the light

    now it's beside the bed,
    when I write "ASSEZ."

[1972]

In the Beginning

The early morning wake-up, melancholia at someone else's radio
                                                        blaring
bittersweet tunes of remonstrable love, in the stuporific lethargy
after rising, fragments of dissolved covert affairs, unresolved
                                ambition in worldly terms and aims
end wonderful instants down fresh clear air rushing in amongst
                                                disturbed embers
throughout crowded past neighborhood apartments, immature
                                youth strivings, illicit embraces,
tumbling headlong to submerge passion, by torrents of chaste,
                                                unchagrined edginess.
Positions dredged that cause shaved identity, though in toto
                        non-surrendered to; perhaps a weekend here,
a fortnight's addiction there, a bar afternoon where
the lights, the clamor, the music combined to erect a home away
                                                        from home,
while still one had one, part shared then afterwards, now
                                                        resurrect to
produce the canopy from careless sophisticated sojourn; yet
                                                        becloudy
the total horizon, as if one did not possessed savor the full means
to find out what he was seeking, and although some permission's
been received, the rough edges — the overall effect's
of unfructified worthiness, and fended *belles lettres*
hoping ungathered future strength results about lost green
                                                        handicaps.

[April 5, 1972]

The Lanterns Along the Wall

Poetry is the most magical of all the arts. Creating a life-style for its practitioners, that safeguards and supports them.

Along the way to becoming an artist are many pitfalls. For those who do not write do not know what true magic is.

Many today become artists by adopting their looks, and gear, or else adhering around or to those who do practice this satisfaction. I cannot imagine a single day, when I have not spent dreaming or conjuring certain habits of the poet. Fortunate the few who are forced into making things surrounding the poets come true. Even though at one time, I believed there would be no reward, for poetic industry and still do, there is immediate response. Things change in proximate location to poetry. There seems to be an aura, or softness as of a romantic glow, or of an enchantment, definitely, as if going back to a children's story, when an adult, or contemplating children. Women possess this nature, when surrounded by their own things, feelings, as a man does, who is within the spell of understanding what is happening to him; they grow wider, broader, and even are able to support a profession and others along with it. Trees are stripped, the sky deepens.

Even oceans, strange from eternity, become more homely with a lovely person, at that moment, within their shore's tides. But does the land belong to the ocean, or the surf? Sunlight, that supports us, contains like proposition.

One must not give up. It could be dangerous and facing a hostile world, to accept in failure.

There is no age for a poet, that he exists outside of time, and is its watchdog. There is love for the strange, the morbid and possessed. We do not give enough joy in our work. Even the act of doing it savors well for the god, but within us and not still to it, must be realized, and attended to as one does infest an absent mind. There is every love for each sensory apparatus, for each one's being. Not as homeless skeletons do await the hospitalized release. There is some love for every loving poet. No man dies loveless.

There are words and they govern. I wrote go on, as infinite aspersions toward the absolute, desired kiss. And I found out, while writing this, even at the risk of putting all my eggs in one basket, that each man does have his own language, particular to himself. It is us, who put the details of morbidness, or perversion upon it.

I can only say real happiness yields from the world of poems. And its practitioners are secret, sacred vessels to an ancient divinity.

And referring back earlier, only I can read my own writing. In the way, it exists in that helio-centric condition around the cosmic orbit.

Poetry exists mainly because of those who practice it. Too often we are reminded that poets are only vehicles for this instrument. It does or does not matter that poets create the art, in dank rooms, or the poet retreats into shadowy places, to call forth the spirits that minister his rhythm or meter. Bearing the repetition, the spirit or substance remains the same.

Unconsciously, or self unknowing, not to confuse the two, preferring the latter, we are instruments for another order, as say, for example, we allow, rather that is to say, let the ancient, over-presuming over trees be our guide. Poets are under magical orders.

They can illumine besides themselves and others, in the moment. Creating infinite allure towards those beings and things they most admire.

The magical descent of sunlight is not more holy than the apparent interruption, though and or despite the need for ever-present human beings to present desires. For who can say what I can say? What more is there to add, except I am very glad to have the backlog or pillow of a previous-achieved poetry, or even poetry being cogitated now, as a form wherein or by I may attain some soft definition of myself.

According to others, as well as to myself, alone. If it's melodious, one will accept it. The continuous provision of goods and food, design, order and loving habits awaits one. I owe poetry for it; it is a pleasure, yes and on the point of contradiction, a reward to work for them, in the ground-level area of good verse. An exciting age perpetuates quality and harmony.

There is a pause in our lives, and to call it loneliness or possession with the minority points of others is no retreat, only reflection.

What comes then to fill the emptiness, or solitariness
Eventually an abundance of beauty and tranquillity.

Within generalized states, as just listed, lies the true presence of what is termed 'white magic.' There are no other forms as far as ultimately I am concerned. No drunkenness can equal purity. Or, other forms, simple address to the prime force of love. Love, not in the sense of kindness or patience, but sometimes trespassed sensual energy.

All these pretensions about the literary life; do they exist, can they be true, by candlelight, or in the small ballroom, under the moon, creeping down between apartment buildings. Yes, poetry is magic, is a pool by which we bathe ourselves, aurally, orally; and what the sound is much closer than one would suspect.

MUTHOS-LOGOS. "The what is said of what is said."
For what we dream does not exist except in our mind.
Or does it? The subterranean rises and creates our reality. May my dreams come true and yours.

The mind-expanding experiences seem to cognate each excitement, that is ours. Not illogically. I have received enough distinction on each one of them, to collate a man's subconscious as equal to the fact, itself. PROPRIO-CEPTION.

Intermittently I lose my family, within my own self. Too little time and too much rest required for reparation of one's energies. I would rather replace them with the peers of my own craft. Any contact with them seems raging and unstable. At other times they are straight and we are on an even keel. It's some interior nature of ours, the whole familial relationship, that determines its beings. I would much rather be with someone else, yourselves, for instance.

Written for Robert Creeley's class of
August 17/72

108

Eila

A pure spirit
her sweater always remains white
smoking and drinking the wine,

Becomes now mid-life
beautiful arms, snow-white hair, face
of the goddess, Aphrodite

pale pearl rose lips
and delicate, in a Finnish voice
she reads my poetry behind tomorrow

night's full moon, in front
of the Hotel, flirtatious as fifty men
ensconced with cheap suppers.

[1972]

Fugitive

Foul wretch upon an ill earth
the suffocated servant claque
bleed unsolicited remark
on every house and hearth

running water to cover ugly thought
from poisoned skin and pest-filled brain,
stretched thieves of black rot,
aiding by impersonated reign.

the bloated sewer songs' domain,
whispered from damned throats
impotent desire from sunken moats
of repulsed prisioners slain

for centuries beneath gutter and stone.
How to expel these bombards giving orders
to citizens unaware they even inhabit
the same nation of rejected aliens in

earnest dread they might seep beside
to take innocence and authority instead
of the noose and nail as apparel cursed
enough for such unnecessary offers.

[1972]

110

Paltry Freedom

Let freedom sing
in this tune or that tone,
let freedom sing
in quick paths and slow.

Let the mind be restored
to its old glow and the wind rung
with old melodies tow
Let there be no resistance

to that dour pealing
of the righteous bow.
Whether to go ahead or stay
at home in memory's boy.

But to offer no recalcitrance
seems paltry
besides that tides outer hew.
The deaf reigning of independence

and the casual sound of this boutique, too.
What one wants to find out is
whether to stray or stay
seems the endurance.

Or to fill the mind with pulsing
reverberations forgotten tomorrow
today's problems now.
How to survive concentrations' stow.

At home the answer lies
when in grace and review one
recaps the unmentioned past anew.
Call this freedom then to view

The three though undefined, as part
subtle linked in one art.

[c. 1972]

Hunger

I keep waiting for him all my life
as an impossible dream I know now with age
shall be delivered; don't all the signs say so,
the rumours prove it. Tomorrow I shall see him,

the real one, and it shall be disappointing. Actual life
shall stand in our way. It's all right for a little while
to torment one, but all your life, to hold me

in a slavery of frustration; it's like some horrible nightmare.
Not war, and its holocaust, for love is the privilege of luxury,
but a terrible yearning as of sexual appetite without nourishment.

Poets should know these things; they're the basic condition of men,
what drives them on, to unhappy homes, constant adventuring,
the simple love between two friends of like profession.
Oh, God, deliver him to my thrusting arms, they bend and break
                    from single greed and selfishness.

[1972]

112

Money Is Not Monogamous

A poor man cannot make use of himself.
He is demoralized through excessive beat exertion.
He cannot take orders even for the good of himself
Usually quite to the contrary.

He surrenders for despair although believes surrounding
                                                    conditions.
He produces fiery revolution in unconscious rebellion.
He believes anything that happens
as misfortune of others.

Quickening as rain on highways, he plunges into chance
faith, duty or conscience culminating legends
of eros, beauty, will & condition
upon distance or parent organization.

He swims with the tide, taking care
he has undressed for it & surveyed its relation
to majority use, freely contributing to its content & current form,
little saving resources toward relentless tides

of time, shallow depths & eventual discharge.
He recognizes none of these fears, not their predicted fact.

[c. 1972]

Playboy

Just think, going to Miami
having the warmth of physical bodies beside you,
gay revolutionist,
        unpinning banners in the kitchen before you leave
    laughing at the poles.
        "Oh this will be easy to carry."

With the lingerie issue of *Playboy* in the knapsack
Just think, seven days without a calendar

And thousands of miles of highways spread out
    before you Bidding farewell to dogs and transient companions

Miami Journal

            July 9, 1972
        as if stepping out of a dream
        we're at highway Exit 9
        Hartford next right
        the sign says N.Y. City

        And oh boy, we're on our way again
        There're four of us, all friends
        from having travelled before, and attending   Liberation
                                            movements.
    Station WORC.
    Passing a truck, labelled Hostess Cup-Cakes

Might as well enjoy the velocity while one can.

In the sunlight and racy wind
Twisting dials to the radio.

Unimperishable beauty.
Allen may have his Himalayas

and I may have my London, someday
through the woods, the ancient unimperishable trees;
that Creeley wept over

114

Time, the day before yesterday

9 Highway stretches as a snake.
Connie Francis "I'm glad that you're sorry now."
Bob driver, a musician confesses he was in love with her
             as a kid, as we were with Judy Garland.

     Maybe my speed is New York City

          I remember sitting in parked cars
               on the Lower East Side
                    so blotted out,
                         I could have been
                              on a roller coaster
Down the valleys
     and into the hills
          by the railway fences
               Passenger cars only 30¢
          Across the bridge and
               over the Tappan Zee
                    through priceless toll gate.

     Now it's New Jersey
          along the weeping willows

through dank-green mud-flats of shallow Delaware river
             the smell of knee-land hay

          Searchlights ahead
          Dusk at Elton
               with blinking highway signals
                    partly up front.

It seems it's Miami
     a Virginia licenseplate racing us
               on the left.
     We've passed fifty thousand cars already.

Who strikes these responsive chords
     as if speeding through glamourous Manhattan.
          The red tailights staying on for miles,
     "Are we in Maryland, yet?"

An imaginary hand rolls up his side-window

Yes, the same boy that rode in the swings at Nantasket Beach
who envisions an auto accident now,
who'd have believed it, is speeding to Miami Bay Beach
for the National Democratic Convention
with his coat and hat spread out around him,
and his bag on the seat, with three companions,
weary before midnight.
One petulant, his feverish corpus looking for release
and the pearls in the hair of another grating
through darkness.

The creepy yellow lights of Washington
our nation's capital,
where its true democratic seats of congress meet together
lost between Massachusetts and 10th Str.

"Temp. in Washington is now 76°."
The radio allows news of our future
to permeate each present.

By the cornices and pillars
5 sleek black limousines patrol
1600 Pennsylvania Ave.,
overwhelming in their earnestness, self-possession and
authenticity, irreduplicatable

I was here in 1970.
Who'd have thought to be back in '72.

"Perhaps we'll be happy again,

somewhere, sometime."

"Where, in the Country of You."

"In dear old Dreamy dreamland"

"When it's sleepy time down south."

The roar of the trucks awaits one

116

After a particularly edifying dream

. . . .

. . . .

transient, Latin temperament and emotional.

Tantric, I notice a strange photograph
                                    in the room
and the book of *Folk Songs of North America*
                                    by Alan Lomax
   I am travelling with an Indian, and it is
                        raining out.

. . . .

   Morning-birds sing in the shaft
                        between two buildings.
Your problems get harder without poetry.
Your friends get fewer.
Times get leaner, and somehow

   waiting here in the A.M.
   for others to rise the morning after seems right.
   It gives a chance to compare things with New York City.
   No such luxury there in a green leather armchair,
   not so many Negroes on streets and in passing cars,
   no fresh breezes and hanging plants off the Potomac

Wall-draped Washington seems serene and compatible
            though there were armed, uniformed police treading
            this hill a few short hours before
                        I noticed

I move out to a stoop, 1819 Vernon St. N.W.
   as a laundry van comes by,
            MAKE MINE MANHATTAN

   I remember their excited rushing feet
      last evening, treading the stairs after sight-seeing the city

         By the steps, planted with ivy and hedges
            cats play now in the long grass
               and a white butterfly dances on wheat thrush

I sense more of ennui from San Francisco
it's as if coming back from a war or
a battlefront beach-head to get well

After two or three years on the scene in different cities.
New York, Up-front Boston and in Buffalo
now in action again, upon Beacon Hill Heights

Out Dancing on the Front Lawn

Two earrings from a jewel-case
with Julie London's old records, last decade
and heartbreaking twilight, from Jan's crash pad
the West End 50's, "make it for one, who's doomed
. . . to join love's refugees . . . and oh, what a castle
leave out the gin."

And just before we leave Bob puts
on John Lennon's new *Some Time* with Plastic Ono Band
very loud
featuring, "Woman is the Nigger of the World."
and I put on my Ecuador hat, made in Italy
with a bar of soap and washcloth under the lid.

"oh, we'll discuss it, someday." A diplomat rides
by in a cab, and the sons of the revolutionaries are
more piggish
than the tricks' Ambassadors from the Dominican
Republic
N W 14th St N W 11th St, "Oh yeah, straight out
and over the bridge."
Tropical palms upon the route. Sizzling road construction fiery
PM
Central American apartment
houses
Coming to New York Ave.   Crossing at walk.

Of all the fifty states, this is the supreme
depository of
statehood and national centrifugicity: leaving it over
The Potomac,   one consoles himself with Wordsworth's *Ode.*
Intimations of Immortality.

118

Uprooted trunks in an open truck
  whizzing blobs of persons
  crushed between smoking foliage.

Faraway young sailors dream of these wooded shores,
    Flashing white teeth, pink in the rearview vizor.
      A second Haynes Pulling Co. vehicle full of roots
        slithering gassy rubber tires

Arolin

    Intermittent flashes of insight
      counteract the coves and summer boats,
        upheld by hi-bred intellectual audiences

      goldenrod slopes stinging the nost-
        rils of Sherman's March to Atlanta,

  Ga. in memory mediocrity including insignificant irritation.

        The scarlet cars flash by
        Orange ones stand still

      Hey, Bob Dylan, what're gonna do with me,
        unattaining mode as single man in mystery.

        Undrugged love remains
        pot history stays out in the rain

          under the speed limit
          Caught by midday up comp.

        IV:

"Ye blessed creatures, I have heard the call
    Ye to each other make; I see
The heavens laugh with you in your jubilee;
    My heart is at your festival,"

        no matter how broken, I do not know
          if the words I sing are mine
            or the voices of my beloveds.

I do not know, if my lover is my brother
or my master. I do not even know
if I have any lover at all;

and that the voices I hear are mine or his.
He has lingered so long in my heart,
I'm sure he exists as a friend

Old farms as tacky queens
wait to take their husbands in
home at darkness.

The last time, rather the first one
I travelled south
I lived in a dream of love,
eighteen summers ago.

It does not seem impossible. The writing does
makes one age, with seasons
or revivifies. Living does not exhaust
one
it's the lack of it gives time its bittersweetness

Huge horseshoe curves open up day's melodies
filling oneself through adventure pushes limits apart
for new crevasses, or potentialities
heavenly cornfields, dense tobacco lumber over the border
through North Carolina,
one may almost smell the Floridaean sea, as on Fifth Ave.
the beauty of writing poetry is knowing it will be read by those
men whom one loves the most
This is not too long
The longer the better for the men who I am in love with.

Naked, sweaty undershirts, puffing on cigars
in political open-window hotel rooms.

Typewriters, brandy, smoke, pills
Even Ed Sanders will have to come to this.
A clearing through the trees
makes one realize, one does not have
an age only vision.

120

And a near-suicide on the parapet above
                causes us to slow down, from the look on his
face.

Ah yes, life is sweet,
      especially if you are heaped with afternoons of boredom,
          You cannot put your old life away,
                especially when a tire skids off
                            the road.
          Two white cars meet without knowing it.
                Jack Spicer denied the real " " ".

Dixie Eberheart's got to read something every so often.

      Oh, my titties feel so good in the wind under this blouse,
      a certain glamour from real poverty glued to ourselves.

In an old Volkswagen sedan hitting 80 miles an hour for
                                    six long hours
      Work at poems is the only permanent, evident release.
      Some only wake to work; others only get up to work,
      some to appear intellectual and despair, they are
                                    contagious
          around a university, breeding stench and filth.
          Columbia, Berkeley, Harvard, Yale.
          They pollute New York, San Francisco, Boston and
                                    New Haven.
      Others wake to play, at sea, on the shore's sand,
      making one think of dancing and life, love at
          Provincetown, and the upper echelons of Sophisticated
          Society, in Berkeley, Cambridge or Las Vegas.

      2)
Then we all put on kerchiefs, and silly hats and bandannas
                                    and pillowcases
      and someone brought out *The King and the Corpse*,
      except for Charlie, who wore pearls in his hair.
The steady drone of motors reminds me of imagined Switzerland
   the true literary principles of H.D. and Swiss emigres
in living European capitals, Marie-Luis Franz
   and Carl Jung, who are more eclectic than we.

121

Red clay Sugar Crk Road brown mud

Kings Mtn.   31   A
                   /artos\

              an abandoned railway car truck van exit
8:35 PM on South 85
$10 SINGLE

    The clenched fist around a crumpled cigarette pack
        Beneath the burgeoning sun's descent
                Absence is failure

    A steam-shovel with a man in the tiny cock-pit up front
      we rattle by, managing useless controls
        beneath the grand sun set.

    And the poem has opened as an
    exegesis of philosophy and contradicting emotions;
    to be contemplated by graduate students
    living in bachelor flats-in-town.

    I miss the lost parts
      I miss the lost poets.
          They are right, the missing gaps,
              as their deaths.

Sonatas to be considered against the whole
            as swamp-lands emit foetid odor before dark
                  on Kings Mtn.
          Outside of Spartenberg
            That Charles mentioned
        in *Anecdotes of the Late War*

    "Weep not, beloved Friends! nor let the air
    For me with sighs be troubled. Not from life
    Have I been taken; . . .
                  —the life which now I live . . .
    Small cause there is for that fond wish of ours
    Long to continue in this world; a world
      That keeps not faith, . . ."

Atlanta 174

with the help of *How Could He Leave Me*
       from The Fifth Dimension

brings to mind that small apartment, left behind
               waiting with the stuffed pillows and mattresses
          "one less man to pick up, after
              all I do is cry."
Can I handle it, since he's been gone
with the low-floor lamp and leather back-rest?

One lone auto
all we have to welcome us
over the shrill, harsh concrete

   crossing into Florida, after the night
spent camping in the state Capitol

of the constituency just left; Georgia

Unearthing old books and feelings,
roaring subway trains, gay Atlanta

Peach lamps and squalid inhabitants,
our buzzing through the border,
just past the state linc.

A few hours more and we'll be at the convention.

    Swamp lilies at the pond.

      Tampa
      Jacksonville
      Tallahassee

In Florida, gulf sands begin to accumulate.
Not bad, for a yokel bus rider.

The delicate sweep of staggering blue morning heaven
                  beneath a bridge
with white clouds etched snow perfection
      grants enough latitude

123

for me to examine his customary perception.
To try and gain fresh condition
less referral to the past
and not thus become an hedonist.

To maintain proper nutrition
against apprehending repetition
The cattle country as green Central park
miraging between marijuana memory
and Arizona jollity

With Mike McClure on the mesa,
outside of Tucson Ghost city
And the cut crops
brimming corn
to bid adieu to
grass land.

Yes, Florida is wealthy as Connecticut is,
true Nevada has been, as upstate Hudson valley,
some emotional correlative.

Blue sleep.

Blue morning

Bayou blues.
FLA S484
Belleview 1 Mile
Cattle gulch.

And the grass is cut, thinned
To a certain length
by the side   of the road.

And the wind has stripped my mind, independent of its will
as a close-cropped range of trees, upon the furthest hill
So that I range back and forth, between now
and myself as a student, writing over a decade
and a half ago.
In the restaurant-cafeteria
I think of the Hotel Commander

124

breakfast, alone for one

he thinks of so many things
that remind him of other things,

A woman in a red hat walks a white dog
through the parking lot, outside,
non-existent geographical situations

non-existent lovers at steering wheels.

2nd Part

Entrance into Miami

The first thing that hits you is

The second

Sun and rain

falling together

in unison

heat lightening

Palm beach shores

great gusts of steam

impenetrable   invisible

Smart Set, smart manners

the things that one learned the hard way
set one apart
as showers let up.

Dilapidated old ranch
under a giant shade
45 miles out of town

Another plantation
    stilling the absorbent intellect
        by unanswered rancor.

    "Some sayd they lovyd a lusty man,
That in theyre armys can clypp them and kyiss them than;"

    If I were alone, I would be out of the car
                    searching along these beaches
    Investigating each one for dramatic possibilities.

"What manner of men set out for these shores,"
        some of the last words left to me

                    lands, ports

        "Travelling down to Miami
        A mile a minute

        Sun shining on Saturday nite

        And when I reach my destiny
        I'm gonna take my life with me
        Searching high and low for freedom"

    Even thinner hands turn down an absent radio dial.

        Vacation-land Frank
    Sinatra of all things, sings, "It Was A Very Good
        Year," who better—rose-canals fuschia
            cherry harbor.

                I created you man.

        In Allen Ginsberg's Darkened Toilet
            At The Albion

    Thursday, July 13th
day of return, two days of revelling
at the convention, marching, carrying banners
protesting, chanting and I am not even a rebel
or radical organizer. Only it's young, and the people I'm in love with

126

are poets and are here, Leroi Jones, Ed Sanders, Charlie Shively
John Giorno. We march together and carry our bags of sand to
                                        build dykes 12 feet high.
    The convention goes on, but we will go home.
                                        To middle-class apts,
and build our world of male imagining. The giant clock outside
                                the window says 8:59 A.M.
    It could be Times Square or Union Square. The lovely light of
                                        Florida
hits the Chinese scroll of work and order upon the wall, opposite
                                the bed where I have slept
thanks to the generosity of Allen and Peter. The church bells
                                chime and the deeds of great men dead
produce labor and striving on our part. Beaches of indolence lift
                                an after noon and morning
out of mendacity, and the clear air, clean wind prompts rhythm
                                        and knowing
to hasten over death and still the fear and painful jealousy,
                                        ravaging boyish hearts.
    Oh my heart is on fire, alive with love for poets.
    As it has always been, no matter what the cause or
                                        condition.
    I see the great building on this island, the flooding lights
                                        of time.
    And know the songs of the rebel organizers and the
                                ardent patriotic slogans
        Of Dave Dellinger and NBC to fall beneath
        The slaughter of memory, to provide for the generosity
            that has always surrounded my place among poets.

    Imamu Amiri Baraka sits in a darkened hotel room planning
                                        for the second
Civil War. I woke this dawn thinking of the innocent dead in our
                                        country
and their senseless slaughter in our streets while Ed Sanders
                                rushes a new book

to deadline, called Vote. The young wait breathless around the
                                nation to make sure their
brothers get through. And they have, at least this time. I am
                                unsure of my
position here. Soon I shall have to leave. Impatience.

                                                        127

And ride back in the car
to Boston. My heart is breaking
    It has been a different world. Miles of human physical flesh
                                                        gnaw
        at my spirit. I delight in sharing group feeling.
            Evening vigils, drag queens, movie actors, marijuana.
            My poem on Miami is done. I have a book of matches, a
                                                            cold
inside Convention Hall, though we marched by enough outside,
                            with the Migrant farm workers.
            John lies asleep exhausted after setting up
                                        Convention Park
with Allen in Flamingo Field nine days ago. I can sense the
                    excitement of the young writing at home for true
historical reports on the scene. I stare at myself in a playsuit in
                                                    the mirror.

    The scroll says: The twelve-fold chain of interdependent
                                            origination.
            Take your father and
                            Mother to task
    for the liberation within our hearts. Scorn poverty and
    seek the plentiful harbors of devotion, wind, sand, sun.

    The smell of left-over marijuana mixed with gasoline.
        A Youth International Party Button 21st St Beach
        and an afternoon on the terrace
            blessing young love.

    New love, encountered between strangers,
    maybe or it's only old love come back.

Miami Beach Nat'l Democratic Convention
July 9th–13th, 1972

128

On a White Cloth

Three loves had I; two men and a woman, in my youth
 one loved me madly, desperately as a child. I cannot forget the
        fire of his kisses; but they
soon cooled, the next, when I left teenage, kept me to herself, in
        taxicabs and smart apts.; oh yes in between
the third a native from Trinidad, how my heart broke on heroin—
                been no one since

Not a look, a glance, a chance, a try or grimace
to lead me on, perhaps an occasional offer, an older man
nothing to match the invitation of my heart, what it yearns for
in adulation from the poets, to lay them low, under that cross

that tribunal. Could one imagine, a book of poems
to be one's master, imagine I say, or the world to be his lover?
It has to be this way. There is no other, to have mastered,
at least the art, one has always sought, of self-expression.

[1972]

Prime Time

for Bonnie Bremser

I've got well again; no more these aches and pains
when sitting down, ceaseless regurgitations; though loveless

the lavish memories taunt what future welfare allows.
Oh sure, there's always music and stolen TV sets, gray mornings

undo this afternoon's good health, traveling in the summer sun to
gas stations.
Of course one has a responsibility to his old friends, though
unfound, and working themselves to death.

One can only pray straight paths continue down 5th street, strict,
unblinking
and that her readings feature The Living Theatre at midnight, for
an incarcerated husband

In Provincetown, also the Toga on Mass. Ave.; the beach bars
abound with perfumed remnants of their countless bodies.
Constant now, before toilets and cruising, Brenda, Washington
debs throw themselves about their townhouses
in testament to your votive shrines.

[1972]

The Loneliness

It is so sad
It is so lonely
I felt younger after doing him,
and when I looked in the mirror
my hair was rumpled.

I smoothed it
and rooted for someone else
or wanted to satisfy myself,
Almost seven,
No hope left.

How can a man have pride
without a wife.

I spit him out on the floor.
Immensely relieved
After ejaculating
Imagining myself up my lover's ass
he coming by himself.

Looking out the window, for no reason
except to soothe myself
I shall go to the bookstore
And pretend nothing happened.
Enormously gratified.

Feeling like a girl
stinking beneath my clothes.

[1972]

Mass.: Verse in the U.S. Since 1955

Since 1955, poetry or verse as some would prefer it be called has, despite all forebodings that it was dying, taken through a handful of writers in the United States, a stranglehold on established modes of thought, analysis, and attention.

Now the secret poet's doctrines of The Holy Grail, the Tarot, especially, and the I Ching, have become popular courses for the inquisitive browser in any chic magazine or Bookstore. Where before Tibetan Buddhism and Zen as well as marijuana and jazz were esoteric pastimes of the wealthy or decadent, they now become scholastic careers for contemporary scientists and priests; i.e., the shopping plazas actually vend handbooks on all these heretofore, only 15 yrs. ago, occult arts.

How has this change taken place?

Mostly because artists read and wrote poems about them, wore their emblems upon their clothing, and incorporated them into their paintings and electronic music titles.

Charlie Parker used mystic titles in his compositions that were known only to the initiated of small clubs on West 52nd St. in NYC, or in bistros of Los Angles, as well as the music halls of Montreal, Philadelphia and New Jersey.

Kenneth Anger practiced magic in his films, *Scorpio Rising, Fireworks*; and the *Village Voice*, first underground newspaper that I know in the second half of the 20th century, began to publish the activities of writers and dancers, who used the off-beat non-commercial elements of our metropolitan cities as more than source material for their art, but in their life-style.

When I moved onto the Hill in 1954, there were a few artists hanging around, always poor and mostly drunk, associating in derelict bars and living quarters. *The Stable* brought in jazz stars and local musicians, for eager devotees. Margaret Charloff had her School of Music, on Boylston St. and still does, I believe. Cambridge was staid.

There were a few good galleries, small ones, Margaret Brown and the ICA. Roger Weber had his bookshop on Chestnut St. but that was conventional and artsy. There was a Poets' Theatre on Palmer St. in Cambridge, right up from where the Coop is now, and a semi Theosophical library nearby. The Theosophical Institute was still based on Commonwealth Ave. But the world at large remained unaware. There was no Committee on the Arts & Humanities sponsored by the State. Inman Square did not exist. The Grolier Book Shop opened its doors to all the young who rushed to frequent it, as *The*

Stable allowed aspiring artists to decorate its walls with murals. *The Sevens* was the gathering place for Bohemians on the Hill, while Cambridge St. was a destitute runway to Scollay Square.

There was a radio show organized by Cid Corman in Boston in 1948-1949 I believe, that programmed what is done here at Stone Soup on Thursday evenings.

What brought art from gallery openings to national educational television throughout the nation? The Museum of Modern Art was built in NYC after the Second World War and the G.I. Bill allowed countless thousands of returning veterans, who had experienced the world in all its mystery and hallucination, to enroll in schools and get paid for it. It was they, I believe, who experimented with leisure and new ideas to force the so-called conventional patterns and norms to be engulfed with more international codes of practice. Existentialism and Abstract Expressionism signaled a new breakthrough.

The die-hards put up a hard fight. Ezra Pound was brought back and sentenced for treason. T. S. Eliot had already become an Expatriate and rejected his land of birthright, becoming a convert to Anglicanism and a citizen abroad. National mores were more ridiculed than accepted as content in serious offerings to an artist's recognition.

It must be remembered as Ezra Pound said that artists are "the antennae of the race." I have never forgotten that one. They see clearer and more ahead of their times.

Since this is my first semester ever, teaching to my own contemporaries, and not to a Freshman English course in Poetry, Prose, and the essay, I hope that you will be patient as we try to go into some of the texts that certainly reinforce the thought that man is more than one, that it is in himself, that his ideas of order and civilization and harmony must occur, rather than in conformist structures of finite logic. That not everything that is useful must be, perforce, good. Or the inverse of what the good is, through religious observance as dictated by foreign, unknowing, uncaring church potentates.

Man does worship the world around him, through himself. Sometimes, not necessarily, in our own times now, the world does not observe man, as exemplified through society. Now we have changed society around and made it observe us. Together we shall plow thru to make room for the little, the unknown, and the ignored.

Besides, as to the fact that there were music bars along Mass.

Ave. but mostly for regular patrons and hard negro crowds, as well as jazz in Roxbury, Folk music was totally, I mean totally, unknown, except to its practitioners, and Folkways Records, that re-issued earlier century classics. As always there were Greenwich Village and Paris.

[1972]

Twenty Hour Ballet

An interview with John Wieners
by Bockris-Wylie

One O'Clock

B-W: Could you trace Olson's influence on you?
WIENERS: He taught me that one was being heard, when he spoke.
B-W: Always to speak with authority?
WIENERS: For the fact that you had listeners. Great poets breed great audiences.
B-W: Yeah.

Two O'Clock

B-W: How about before Olson?
WIENERS: Before Charles, I practised a hands-off policy in terms of my experience.
B-W: With that change, did the actual physical aspects of your writing change?
WIENERS: I was looking inwards, rather than gazing out.

Three O'Clock

B-W: Why is so much of your writing about being alone?
WIENERS: Actually I want someone else to be there with me.
B-W: Do you?
WIENERS: Always.
B-W: Really? Is that a True Confession, John?
WIENERS: Yeah.

Four O'Clock

B-W: So you're not alone that much now.

WIENERS: Well, have I gotten it straight that the reason for isolation should stem from a sense of desolation?

B-W: They usually walk hand in hand. When you're happy you're with more people.

WIENERS: My heart just skipped a beat.

Five O'Clock

WIENERS: I don't have any objects in my poetry.

B-W: Shall we bring out the text, professor? Shall we start quoting?

WIENERS: Yes. What ones do you seize upon?

B-W: *Nerves* is very object-oriented.

WIENERS: Because of the bric-a-brac.

Six O'Clock

B-W: This is supposed to be an interview about craft and poetry.

WIENERS: It is! It is!

B-W: It's also about the craft of conversation, which is interesting. You're really an expert conversationalist.

WIENERS: To my own detriment.

Seven O'Clock

B-W: This poem: "To sleep alone/ to wake alone/ to walk alone/ to wash alone . . ." What started you off writing that? Were you in your apartment?

WIENERS: Yes.

B-W: In bed?

WIENERS: Yes. Before midnight.

Eight O'Clock

WIENERS: Mary Butts is another prose writer I admire.

B-W: Mary Butts?

WIENERS: Yes.

B-W: Mary Butts? Must you be obscure?

WIENERS: The Congressional Record. Is that prose? Reference books of all types.

Nine O'Clock

B-W: Do you need someone who would inspire you?

WIENERS: Someone who would question the point of my existence.

B-W: Have you ever fucked and thought "I've got a great poem!" and hurried out of bed?

WIENERS: Yes, searching for paper and related materials.

B-W: I guess we all have the same experiences.

Ten O'Clock

WIENERS: Well, how much fucking have you done?

B-W: This is "The Craft of Poetry"? We've covered the field, Mr. Wieners, both here and abroad, in various zones, shapes, both male and female and in the guise of animals or whatever, a few cats, a couple of rats . . .

WIENERS: We can stop, I think, using sex as a tool for poetry.

Eleven O'Clock

B-W: Do you take politics into consideration?

WIENERS: Well, if you were working for the *Times* . . .

B-W: But you're not. We're asking you.

WIENERS: What if one wanted to?

B-W: Do you want to?

WIENERS: I do.

Noon

B-W: Ungaretti told us, "I'm not looking for the beautiful, I'm looking for the precise."

WIENERS: I value the beautiful more, or as much as the precise. I put the precise within the terms of beauty.

B-W: Have you noticed a beauty in fear?

WIENERS: Yes, I have.

138

One O'Clock

WIENERS: If hatred is aroused through an act of poetry, how or what do you explain or do about it?

B-W: You either decide the hatred is misguided, or the poetry is misguided. Do you discard poems on the basis of audience reaction?

WIENERS: Twenty-five percent.

Two O'Clock

B-W: In Gerard Malanga's Paris Review interview, Charles Olson was a reserved elder statesman.

WIENERS: That's facile! Charles thrived on flattery.

B-W: Do you dress the part?

WIENERS: If I had more money, I wouldn't be allowed to go out on the streets.

Three O'Clock

B-W: Nature.

WIENERS: Health.

B-W: Airplane.

WIENERS: Tenderness.

B-W: Dream.

WIENERS: Realised.

Four O'Clock

B-W: How much respect do you have for intellect?
WIENERS: Above recognition. Recognition is repetitive. Poets' intellects don't matter as much as their having arrived in poetry.
B-W: When does someone arrive in poetry?
WIENERS: When he's able to be taken advantage of.

Five O'Clock

B-W: Do you take care of movie stars once they're inside you, or do they take care of you?
WIENERS: That's . . . very good. Because through adopting their dress and style, you're doing both.
B-W: I almost always put on a pair of pants when I write.
WIENERS: Because you have a big dong, that's why.

Six O'Clock

WIENERS: The point of no return annoys me the most. Being alone annoys me the most.
B-W: Mr. Wieners, what is "The Craft of Verse"?
WIENERS: A form of the active function.
B-W: Have you ever been interested in interviewing anybody?
WIENERS: I would find it quickly boring.

Seven O'Clock

B-W: What is the happiest incident in your life?
WIENERS: I suppose the happiest work I've done is beyond the point
          of my life.
B-W: So it didn't take place? It wasn't on Route 66 at 7:00 p.m.?
WIENERS: It hasn't been for some time.

Eight O'Clock

B-W: When you're angry, you speak two inches higher in your
          head.
WIENERS: Well, I once thought that. I said it to somebody.
B-W: What does a big house mean to you?
WIENERS: Eternity. I also like other people's eyes, by the way.
B-W: Thank you darling.

[1972]

We Would Be Two Men

After eleven years
of ambition and frustration,
rejected
expending desire on poets,
to end up
attending readings, giving benefits,
burdened by malnutrition,

a strange fire burst between
myself and a dark-eyed man,
who was married but whom I later
discovered to be my husband;
a gentleman skilled in business and letters.

He is wealthy, gay, and drives cars,
having accomplished achievement
in theatre, music, and medicine.
He travels from continent to continent
at times accompanied with woman and children,
addressing no one but myself.

Lost in his arms for two days,
I find my secret passions rewarded;
melting, blended as before
receiving kisses as from a king of
                    The Black Sea,
no one able to compete with his necessity.

[1972]

Jimmy

I suppose that's how I was born,
Come on and go down on me,
because I live in misery
far away from the sea.

And the joy riders moan painlessly
beside the seat of justice forlorn,
without tea and revolutionary,
on that crowd bird of fancy.

I aint gonna live on welfare,
I am Grace Kelly
and I was meant for corn,
before you, Nelly

Sharp ever came into the country,
you may only betray by
guns and thievery,
not to mention razor's horn.

They call them Orestes,
They don't own me,
I support them and the China torn
through Russian treachery.

I'm your Jeanne Cagney,
They used to call me
                    Jeanne
with the light brown hair shorn
by a one-eyed thievery.

They kill any
man who loves me
                    suddenly
from the colored area
I suppose that's how I
                    was born.

　　—(Bob Dylan

[1972]

It Was Yours

I'm a bigtime baby now
with a place all to my own
and a refrigerator light

that's always going
golden glow
when for morning's slow
I open its door for cheese and dose.

oh my clothes, the constant blows
from town and mose who bow
and close, to know this
suppose.

[1972]

Song

I had a room in Buffalo
oh oh oh
and it had a cathedral window oh oh
   overlooking a courtyard, so
into it, I do come and go

to get well from New York City snow
when the winter winds did blow
oh oh
and all I saw I noted below.

From start to finish slow
my world was definitely a one-man show.
In that little room of Buffalo,
my friends would stand in a row

where did they all go,
above and over the rainbow; oh oh
my room has a different tenant now
while I live past the meridian zero

It was real spooky there, though
the walls were peeling yellow
and once coming through the door, too
I got hit by a bolt of lightning blue.

Girls stayed with me and boys, few,
we changed our dreams and melodies true
and tough they died, at least some,
                I keep the mantle askew
To welcome them into my heart, anew

Within my little room in Buffalo,
four years of my life did go, oh oh
as surely as time upon the calendars mow
but in the life of a room, what does that grow?

Sweet and low
I'm really up to it now
since I moved away and became another fellow,
though my room's memories follow.

[1972]

Two Men

As a popular song on the phonograph, by Laura Nyro
or in crowded bars on Saturday afternoon, these men came to
                                                                        mind;
or as gradually turning on the lights in your apartment
during daylight, the glamour of their bodies
and their persons filled every longing of his mind.

It could be the chime of a cathedral bell, raising his
spirit that he saw them, in their own particularity.
The oldest was Robert, he was only forty-six at this
writing and he had one eye. He was world-famous and had
married two times before this last separation. He was a writer
                                                and possessed, as the other,
the quality of high-speed roadsters. There was an internationalism
about them, of sleek music and dark cafes. They frequented the
company of women but he, this narrator, loved them anyway.

Harvey was thirty-six and immensely wealthy. He was blond and
god-like. He was married and had three children. He lived in
the country and published a small press of ignored documents in
American culture. At this time he was ridding himself of drugs,
fashionable from the decade before this one. A certain aura of hot
jazz permeated any contemplation of his body. He had good looks
and a joviality that always led one on to peruse the fact that were
circumstances a bit different and the occasion right, one could
                                                have ended
up in bed with him. He had a series of mistresses and supposed
casual love affairs, concealed from his wife.

[1972]

146

Drug Fantasy

international homosexual
                  playboys

wide open feelings of summer

wide open feelings of summer

one may love but never get married
and learn to discard other human beings lightly

for death is the death of love
an affair, yes but never too seriously
though tears are shed.

                  The dank, glamorous
feelings of sub-altern caves and smoky candlelight
can become boring, long indigo fingernails, oh how arch, so refined

  Death also for a lover,
    tragedy
             the ripest fruit
                  of the sweet.

And you, —
             sit waiting for me
                  at home, in some cafe.

             That is the way I want it to be,
                  Melancholia,
                      self-sacrificed passion.

Let hordes pass by, unnoticed
uncaring on rough stones by giant hotels.
At the beach, we will bronze ourselves
for the supreme moment of love, abandoned from a balcony.

        Speeding cars, dark glasses, close-coifed hair, the
        dazzling smile—all create the general illusion

147

of having so much to offer, that promise rejected by the
deed.

Travel long distances, journey to foreign ports,
the eyebrows oiled, raised at the proper height

make chance departures, timed to offend your audience
most.

[1972]

Nudes

To The Museum of Modern Art

The glimmer of sunlight
upon the silver cover,
as the dervish dancers
last evening of Turkey

George or Tom Wesselman, Edward
Weston's bare torso; Arthur Davies'
A Thousand Flowers and Sitnikov
gives us something to talk about over coff-

ee & brandy at least. yes, Art beacons the street;
not "Art on the town," as a byword for compen-
sating oneself to enthusiasm. Exhuberance, energy—
A *birch tree* has a naked man stretched to its limbs
amid the foliage, above a summer meadow. Leaves serve
as skirts yesterday, an evanescence of heaven. Non-being

through many forms within its sphere. Twentieth century art
provides the disillusionment of a century. It holds the jagg-
ed pieces and bits of many visions to the viewer. Many personal

experiences recorded through a photograph. Henri Cartier-Bresson's
untitled lovers upon a silk coverlet brings to mind ecstasy from
the future.

What one has rejected from the dark woods spring dances at school

and summer convention in Berkeley.
A man's skin is his own. His majesty. What an honor
when another human wishes to touch it and deposit
within it his nature's gifts. Tendernesses of love do

not disappear, they build calendars, appointments, notes
as a book in the October morning to catch the
sunlight glimmering through a tenement window,
when two people meet, or three, or four as some record of will.

[1972]

Poetry and the Social

Summer days are really over. Bleak winds
seep over the Hill, whipping memory through
forgotten parties at the peak of harvest moon.

Delayed acquaintances desert suburbs in favor of warm
matinees, furcoats, heavy glasses, storms wipe
snow tires ascending plateaus precipices,
autumn's leaves break as minds bristle, wild dogs howling

in abandoned yards under lanterns. Steam verse
really makes the scene in warm jackets, peacoats out of
Mickey Finn
"My life has gotten pretty absurd at this time, so anything
goes, especially if it's free"

    The parisian gossip goes far
but not far enough to stand for bogusish
at this time; work has created a period of intensity
in face of youth. Duane Locke does not hold water,
for this night's full moon shouts imperatives
to Jack Spicer's snowman and David's bareass sculpture.

    Local politics, hoodlums, call girls all seek
        fire in words, "brown weeds everywhere . . ."

[1972]

150

At the Carnival

Marriage is a joke; is a laugh
when men can't even keep faithful to their spouses;
Why should they; and yet those words of trust espoused at the
altar.
The women know it, too. Keep their legs open, just in case

Perhaps it's two people who set up an arrangement. Might as well
make a pact with a bureau knob. There are aspirations to the
moon,
    to the north star, to mountainous valleys that are more
important.

And when I think of you, the plains of old world nations come to
mind
against this bar, where I am now, forlorn.
The old world *ethos* thrills my heart: obtuse, covert

how can you keep tract with someone not merely more than a
housekeeper
no matter how intelligent When I want to dance and proclaim
my acquisition as cocktail lounge . . .
with craft, amid bottomless channels of familiarity.

Without obvious terms of contract, lover, girl and husband.

What use could I make of myself except this importunation . . .
obscenity or become a perpetual bar-fly?

[1972]

The Pool Hall

in an abandoned toilet,

did the lights still work,

the asylum was a barracks, in the next building
that's where they keep them in Front and Center,
                                    he could just see
        EC 6 and EC 8, did they flush

the Broadway feelings porch, the desolate tone of derelict hotels,
peeling walls, absent telephone, posted notices no one read,

unremembered trophies, an empty soap dish

  The long, narrow halls, unopened doors
     and striped red and green forlorn streamers from a forgotten
                                        festivity

How the wind blew in May, with cracked ledges
past the bars, stone cold, could it be old memory

                   was keeping another cold potato to
                      rustle up an ancient scene,
                   venerable, hearing rain upon eight foot screens?
                   and an empty cup for cigarettes,
                                   of water.

[1972]

To Labor, Power and Energized Devotion

M'sieu Paul;

How I'd love to be with you and think of you, watching you on television, with your wonderful sense of humour, beneficence, generosity, and patient thoughtfulness. Without you, love or life seems somewhat futile, set in place by words alone. Of course, without you, as you know, love only is possible to keep solidarity, with your elegance, demureness and sobriety.

Your wonderful face as Lawrence Harvey is filial strength to my chain of interest. You know I could not be separated from you. Over these terms we have long pondered. With both my parents dead I am terrifically endowed now as strength of wealth, singly rears its consoling gear to hip my temptations, in your direction of rescue, efficiency and legality.

Your police experience allows me now to rest easier, without narcotics, as history attests. I have never been their slave. I immediately went home to Mother Superior for treatment, if the strain of government overcame my tempered responsibility, acquired by dutiful respect to monies, disease and parsimony.

She as my Own Mother treats me from heaven, no matter if it it a LEPEr's one, though I know her beauty as supreme in the gentle tones of education, allegiance and permission for my spend-thriftiness, discord and woe-begoneness.

As the years wend on, we renumerate one another. Unbeknownst to me, until reflection, as my chief advisor beside yourself, we could never garner our private sunny afternoons and trust, in all materials.

Worth to you to remember, how gracious she is and has been over countless holocausts in my doubt, from your contraband at times awareness.

While working in verses, I have dreamt of some idealization from a protector as yourself, who hears my every thought, and recognizes each word, both from the past, and might predict the future out of syllables, vowels and repetitive consonants. You would call these friends from language as possessors of the gift of prophecy.

153

I do not begrudge it to anyone who pushes such allocation for my self. It helps to serve them and our trails from the law-maker legislators and superior judges.

As the Supreme Court, himself, these tri-partite attorneys or one may say attuned representatives should keep that office holy, pure and good. Not trying the petty, bourgeois, or beanbrains who popularize lore, legacies and libelousness, adjacent to each commander of legions, lummox'd through exposed guidance. How else may peculiar salvation acquit two decades discipline and destined acquaintance to forces, that suppose aesthetic zeal.

We keep enchanting assignations, a breakfast, western shore, valley ranch. Sanctity, support and the simple treatment class charge stamps.

[1972]

The Cut

After Reading Gerard Malanga's Interview with Charles Olson
in The Paris Review, *Summer 1970*

Only an hour to write this
on an Allegheny Airline into Syracuse
the trouble with magazines is they provide no space
to write in, as opposed to books

down below, the earth appears as the most
priceless jewels ever unearthed,
diamonds as big as watches
on the elegant wrist of Connecticut
Why is it a major poet seems impossible
to write about, while the ingratiating success yields
odes of dazzling elegy & national award

Charles, I have little words to suppose
before your image; the shadow of night clouds & fog winds
bounce us as a marble in pitching pennies

and why anyone is fool enough to fly these small planes
out of Boston on a Friday evening the 1st of December,

one of your favorite dates; Moonset, Gloucester) 1972.
Art is more than a matter of natural idiosyncrasy;
you were the godamnest biggest meteor to crash across
    these skies
since see above

if one could suppose nature before his birth.
You talked; how they talked; you were not alone.
You needed

and all one conceded he could do
to listen; some talked back; some contributed,
if even punctuation marks, were noted.

Not a wave broke, was measured, nor cumulus
formed, but viewed; not leaf fell, got retrieved.
Not a woman past, unloved, not one eye filled
was addressed.

[December 1, 1972]

Plane, train, car, bus, or boat

along the coast, seabreeze
slopes sunny Beacon Street
    serene March elms, in like a lamb my mind

1973, four years under black cloud—
was it from Charles' first letter to the asylum?
It must be, for now Fanny Howe-Sena

lifts his pall, meeting after hokey reading at BC;
in the South End Library, for Bill Corbett's,
no, it's not pure ambition—the carriage of an Irish

woman through his study, identical to my cousin
though of different faith & social rank, Geraldine, lifts
his simmering rage off my head, awaking this morning,

for more of thought than Celtic beauty, her blond visage J.P.
permits peace upon Beacon Hill, from her place physical jane
perfume drifts two decades in azure as Tristan or Isolde.

[1973]

The Keyholer

My dear, do you mind if I strike a flint upon your

boxwood smcars veneer

just in time for dildoes

with a crush of red shoes

and nail polish
out of Moira Shearer's
childhood bayonet morning
named Anna K. Gibboneer

Christian Dior scarlet milquetoast toes.

Most slaves bear tarnished
broken fixtures future
second-hand readies to wear.

[1973]

New Beaches

Poverty has nearly ripped my life off,
kept me on the streets and in boarding houses,
drove me into asylums and maddened drug-addiction
tenements, where I lost my mother and father.

Kept lovers in my mind, some how they did not help
against beggardry the sun shine outside did
even still the hag of toothless poverty waits behind the kitchen
    door
a future uncertain as ever, although I cannot afford to lose my
    sense of its past

It was only poets who helped me, and their sponsors needed me
half-a-decade of rest, the skin on my legs has changed it holds
    together
now as a rich person by itself, I have vowed I shall never be poor
    again and know
I shall never be lonely again, because of the love that dwells
    within poetry's mouth.

[1973]

To Those of Born Divine

I see each day as a miraculous present,
not of poetry but being
this morning I dreamed and last evening
the horrible ascent to a ferried height, terrifying
both facts I wish to as a Tibetan coney deny this afternoon and of
                                   Robert Duncan's versifying

in my own permanence, and to assert
pertinence against what forces beat
out particularity and individuality.

Yes, death in life is a loud flailing
around sun flowers, who rise through their own eagerness
uninvoluntarily over burnt embers of another inhabitation.
Past conflagration, new contingence.

What are dreams, who are ladies
the Muses seem as remote as that State House
Commonwealth Capitol dome, even before new curtains are hung

and shades of post-noon reflections a shade of
reality above Magnavox drones.

Spare me from these unconscious messages.
Why are they so important.

Beyond the street congress
and house hold scents rising in answer
to burnt wishes. From whence

do the drives, obedience within mankind,

spring competition; propagation or
individuation? Life in the twentieth

              century is a complex
decision, arising out of new information,
      facts and self-proven success.

Not only portents, or omens,
    occult deliverances
that teat, teat away at these original occurrences

from meeting, mating, travel.

And if I fail to unravel
  last night's or this morning's messages
  should I suffer in amiss
at my necessity to live where fire burnt, also.

[1973]

On a Fats Navarro Record

Under a neon light
the same two rumpled pillows that confine
my world in the evening

a mirror for the sleeper, alone
as he creates an history towards the future
yet do we not all turn

as one single heritage, post master
and grandfather, dreaming in eternity
past midnight tune of isolate requisite?

[1973]

Audience of One

At last we have all arrived
behind a silver diesel
                    in a clubcar

right down the street
from where we started
                    proceeding East

                    preceding West

Pfut. In the morning light
the red coat, gold angel, evergreen tree
                              denote another Christmas
                                           season
across the room from where
I placed the roses last evening
                    in front of your photograph.

At last we have now all arrived
from where we wanted to go
                         to end up in the morning light, half
naked, waiting for breakfast
                    and "the man I love" to come down

from heaven and answer our pleas
of where we wanted to go
                    other than dreams, other than within
                                        your arms.

The track we ride upon, the ego
we wish to submerge, at last
                    one with change, one with Hermes.

[1973]

162

"God Is the Organ of Novelty"

A. North Whitehead

In negligences resulting out of poverty,
where hypocrisy may be confused as Malthus
too rigid devotion either visually against society
in pursuit of favor from idolatrous persons—

the art of yesterday's mutations throttle propriety,
horizontally, less classical reformations' gains
in terms inherited without examination, labor pains
forcing amnesia, even jealousy to minor proportion.

Bullionaires pass as quarry without guards, in guilt
hoping to please an artist and his proprietor, twin
judges before a capital demonstration without stint,

being brought up on conscious intoxication that fortune
plays both sides rush or cease without regard to flint,
that rather unflinching search for ends to meet.

Prices collapse upon inspection, where trust burns
energy out either for the weather upon four walls;
a gallery courtyard harassed through invention.

[1973]

A Superficial Estimation
of
an English Lady
a Mexican Lady
a California Lady
a New York Lady
a "Polynesian" Lady
&
a Massachusetts Lady

Elizabeth Taylor is my sister. You might as well know it. And as you might know, she is always with me, even though married to someone else. I recently visited them at their home on Cape Cod, where they have a small house, piquant in its quaintness against the woods of Duxbury, Massachusetts. It is large and spacious, true and blue, under the oppressive clouds of August.

My sister is a generous woman. Never once in the thousand times we have met has she refused me anything. Of course, in an imposing question, she is confused. And with funds, she is thrifty. But in matters of generosity, you may be assured she shares in a human, impulsive fashion the dictates of my will.

Christmas, Thanksgiving, Easter, birthdays, holidays are always observed. She is ever faithful and will not deny the triumphs of her career in her personal dealings with others. Though often insulted by the mediocrity of contemporaneous activity, she peruses her surroundings with dignity and harmony no matter what the crisis.

At the end of the Second World War, and at its onset, she was horrified and overjoyed. Too much sorrow over death has ripened her maturity to a steadfast passivity, at times ununderstandable to anyone but her closest family relation, mother and myself. Her father of course plays a crushing role in her concern. Nonetheless, in a religious experience she must reject him.

Until I see her again, of course, I harness my own reserves towards a perfection of my talents, neaping the qualities of tidiness, dutifulness, and propriety in the event she may interpret the situation favorably.

Until of course public appearance demands, as it must, our conduct in town, I recall why yesterday she left such a favorable impression in my mind while showing a visitor from California the delights of Cambridge, in its hustle, bustle and traffic contradictions. We parted and Elizabeth came into the Pangloss Bookshop

164

with her husband, with the most lovely coiffure and ensemble. Of course we had passed on the cobblestones earlier and I had mentioned to my guest, that the body we had just passed I had spoken to backstage, at the Schubert, after the performance, in a new Pulitzer prize-winning hit, now on Broadway at the Alvin Theatre.

I was in the process of purchase, and of course, as the transaction completed itself, through the skilled hands of the clerk at the desk, I spoke to Miss Taylor, about her eyes and complimented her on their unforgettable blend of walk-plot ordinaries and trellis welcomers. She was more than delighted at my praise of her virtues and we passed fifteen minutes together in browsing. Needless to say, she did not purchase anything. We left separately.

*   *   *

Rita Hayworth, tight-lipped as always, sat in her living room chair this evening with obvious relief, for the bus ride from Boston was an exciting, exhausting, enervating event. She looked at me with the dark, flashing eyes of desire that have haunted the film screen ever since I first saw her, in the manner of Ava Gardner in *One Touch of Venus*, in *Gilda*.

Regarding *Lady from Shanghai* for its graphic representation of linear structure, I knew that kind of beauty would never die no matter how old she was, as I, post-sunset.

We sat and exchanged briefly our news of the day. Too tired to stay up, she went to bed and I came down here to work on letters and business obligations, pausing now at 3:48 Eastern Standard Time to remember her as I know her in person after worshipping her in *Miss Sadie Thompson*, *Fire Down Below*, *Cover Girl*, *Pal Joey*, and *Affair in Trinidad*.

She has always been a girl after my own heart, and no one more skilled than she in show business. She knows how to put on account, give one, and continue her performance after the role's end. She is gay, witty, brilliant and full of the sparkling effervescence necessary to keep a man's interest alive. Hearing her tonight I was reminded of what I have always wanted to be—a gossip, a behind-the-scenes man who knew all the stars, was able to enjoy their carryings-on, and to participate in the difficulties of experience in our contemporary society.

How many times I have been a guest in her home is impossible to recount. Day by day we have been together and the love within my heart grows stronger with each passing intimacy.

The demands of being a star are inexorable. Twenty times a day in the city, no matter where they are, I have always been occasioned to her devotion, her patience in the face of my attempts to conduct myself as an adult. In Boston, New York, San Francisco, and Cambridge she is always there as my friend, lover, father, sexual object, sales person, model, princess, and advisor. Without her my life would be lost.

My letters to her contain mostly complaint, and hers to me, warm devotion. She forever extends and guards over my difficulties, in traffic, commerce, and acquisition. Interstate Commerce Commission. Her brightness, availability, and encouragement. Maintenance, three to four thousand people a day.

With this tribute to her intelligence, forethought, and advancing strength, I have only realized the total adoration and hypnosis I am subject to every moment I see her on screen, and off. From the moment she is photographed to the unending desire she generates within me as audience, and transmitted from herself, I remain a passive slave to her wishes, knowing I'm unnecessary to her.

* * *

Imitation of Life, where Lana Turner is "married" to a fortune-hunting Hugh O'Brian, amidst the palazzos of Los Angeles and the cabanas of Acapulco, yields in actuality a rather dead end to any citizen wishing to duplicate their frustrated actuality.

How simple Lana becomes in *Madame X,* when she confesses her hospitalization, after a Swiss honeymoon, actually filmed in an area outside of Rochester, New York. Toytown, U.S.A. False snow, false jodhpurs, everything except the role's gore is false.

We see her in her "Mexico City" hotel, high on absinthe, actually the Greenwich Village Hotel, and in a small cafe previously, discussing the possibility of intercourse in the Earle Hotel, Waverly Place, New York. A delightful place to stay and catch cold. Honeymoon suite included.

* * *

Now, looking for work. Why hasn't anyone heard from Barbara Stanwyck these days? From my impresson of her last evening in Plymouth at the theatre, she is a watchful, ever-abundant woman, with the greatest sympathy for the sensitive, easily

166

oppressed individuals in our society. She is plain attractive, queenly and dignified, in complete attention to her surroundings, and she imparts that quality of motherhood and concern so missing in our ordinary affairs.

Without Robert Taylor she may be lonely. Has her career been enough to sustain her, or does she look to her investments for gratification? A book of her achievements in the theatre and on film would aid us in understanding the fixation she plays in our imagination.

I, at times, imagine myself to be surrounded by her devotion, preferably favorably, for I keep house now for my father and myself and my late mother's family, and I'm pleased to know she is in the vicinity, perhaps actively involved in politics and employment. From my observation of her behavior in public one could only benefit by her proximity.

A stunning visage, a careful coiffure, a healthy optimistic attitude towards action, a positive gait, a determined at times mind, and a total gaiety. As my godmother, she has been overly generous and I have never repaid her through card or present. Only recently I bought her an umbrella, turquoise, for she likes bright colors against a rainy heaven, and she shyly entered my bedroom at my request and accepted a small token. It was the only place I could choose to present her with the present, as her sisters, my aunts, had filled the living room and kitchen with their industrious aid in writing sympathy cards after a recent funeral, as had my sister. I met Maureen Connolly in South Boston, too, during a wake, and she had that obedient uprearing that gratifies my own moral desires.

Miss Stanwyck and the friends and co-workers she associates with are sensitive and law-abiding. Their names are Adele Jergens (hair concern), Marie MacDonald (body work), Bonita Granville (face), and Carol Baker (hands). They handle the grooming of the performers. When I sat before Miss Stanwyck and her four stars, one seat over from Barbra Streisand, and two from Elizabeth Taylor, my sister, I felt I was in the theatre as old, with the magic delight of song and figure, transforming myself, the ghost of decades back, to the appearance of a forgotten prince, humming the tunes with the performers, with no irritation expressed from Bette Davis, sitting in front of me, on Betty Grable's shoulder, or Kim Novak, one seat to the right, who hopped in late with Jennifer Jones.

The Austrian aristocracy has not declined. We all sat there, the Empress and I, the stars, the foreign accents, the shifting profiles, the glancing eyes, the telltale brows, and the form of experience became elegant, enraptured, and carved as if from Thomas Edison, with the postures and movements, gestures and positions of well-ordered monarchs, all assuming courtesy and consideration towards those who profess eagerness to share in the virtue of art.

*　*　*

Now, Dorothy Lamour is one of the strongest women I have ever met. As my Aunt Marion, she has been an example of success and ambition personified. Always well-groomed and simply dressed, in harmony with inherited fashion, she possesses the most elegant and stately carriage of my relatives, all of whom—Marlene Dietrich, Ava Gardner, Bette Davis, Betty Grable, Elizabeth Taylor, Hedy Lamarr, Lizabeth Scott—have fantastic bodies, healthy hair, interesting and timely hands, and delicate feet. Their work in the films has not gone unrewarded. They are known the world over.

Miss Lamour this evening was thoughtful and professional as at each occasion we have met, the past eight years. She is Washington-based in her dedication to national pride, is loyal and rooted in true participation in social affairs. Her cuisine of native recipe and devoted zeal yields nourishment of ultimate strength. Without her taste of plain accessories, exotic costume, and glossy macquillage, my sojourn in town, in Metropolis, would vanish into bleak ennui. She has raised her citizenship to patriotism of the most homely nature, and delights in anecdote with vague and unexpressed narrative. Her permissiveness is regal, her embrace unforgettable, a stirring experience untouched even by her own nephew, and as I have never consciously written of her earlier, I now wish to record how sincerely leading her image throws ahead my direction to be a good person, a country's leader, a royal monarch, in a fashion dictate to myself, and to my audience's attention. My ambition always was to be looked up to, to be admired, congratulated, and loved. I take it for granted people like me, and if they don't they are bad people, or dissatisfied with their condition.

My Aunt Marion, Dorothy Lamour, works for herself in career profession, in capability to its required functions, and overcompetence in choice of objets d'art, furniture, and proverbs. She has old-fashioned taste, an air for cruises, a sensible ensemble of devotees, and a genuine worship of gods.

*　*　*

168

My mother, Bette Davis, was the most generous woman I have ever known. She tended to me day and night for over 35 years, seeing to my every wish, my ordinary needs and wants, providing all emergency seclusions, and creating a person without doubt towards equal any distraction would offer. She pervaded every occasion, helping increase its significance, conduct, importance, and satisfy the intention of its occurrence.

She gave, 24 hours a day, tremendous meaning to herself, myself, her house, the rest of the family, and the world outside, delighting especially in beautiful people, delicate materials, and serene surroundings, admiring the weather, facts, neighbors, their improvement in family growth. Her diligence in diet obvious, her care in housework overconscientious, her admiration for society overwhelming, and her interest in acquisition eager and exhausting. She purchased for us every year necessary clothes, sent us to school daily, made our lunches, paid our bills, cleaned our rooms, dusted our books, replaced our overlooked possessions to their proper places, saw to our idiocies, indulged in her own pleasures, and entertained by party and phone our friends' political aspirations and plans.

Now in her empty room her perfume bottles, vanity chest, lamps, and jewelry boxes stand, a national music to motherhood and maternal vigilance. With her gone, I must keep the windows clean, the floors dusted, the furniture polished, the bathroom shined, free of marks and smudges, the refrigerator full, and the pans clean, as would be her work. For you see, my mother was all I had, all I needed to go on, out in the world, to be a success, to make a name for myself and keep our honor up. Untarnished in the face of all those who would tear it down and besmirch her with any accusation of tawdriness or unfaithfulness.

Her patronage externalized each day of the week, evening, morning, and afternoon. Distance meant little, and she could travel well to any part of the globe by phone or car, bus, train, and boat. She used the mails daily, and looked and spoke with enthusiasm of the postman, newsboy, and express delivery. Home freshness a necessity, and the lawn had to be cut and the hedges trimmed and the snow shoveled, electricity used and phone rung, the trees strong and flowers gay and bushes perennial.

Her wishes for her children would be they always were happy, and her prayers Sunday directed to that purpose. Her hopes in political leaders, they were handsome, and in actors the same. But not that they were overwhelmingly so, from the screen. And she loved a good show, a great musical.

Shapely legs, fine bosom, well-kept permanent, always done by the week, and beautiful eyes, as in the case of my sister Elizabeth Taylor. She loved girls more than boys, though I've heard her deny this, most of her friends, showed an enthusiasm towards older women. She was overly shy towards any man, though not in my case, ever reticent, ever unable to express her phrase, from knowledge of animals, racial types, and especial accents. She had a good ear, could dance well, sing excellently, and habitually cooked, making cakes, puddings, pies, brownies, cookies, jellos, stews, and friends, in diminishing faith. She tired easily and showed it, became ill easily, expressed it, and left many looking after her, as they had come to her in radiant blossoming, towards her intelligence and I think, no, fairness.

[1973]

Adult, To His Inspiration

Thank you for showing me your insides, Johnny,
for staying with me all day
for being good to look at with me

precisely where I cannot afford to live perhaps
hesitatingly painfully aware I could not sit without a visit, above roofs in front of elegant river

Set-ups   a calla-lily easter
                                    the kyrie orizen
bringing Charles to the sill
                            blue main retinue

Frank only wrote skyscraper poems, yet he never had one, down
                    town E, Ninth walkup that I robbed once
                            of a disastrous residue
never spoke of again, the Broadway town-house below
            with its armorial throne, a "loft" as he told my mother
            even on Mass Ave. swank penthouse

        but never this

                    view!

        for miles out to sea, the staggering Robeling

            conceptual, aerial union amid

        yellow Cornish coal, could coral hibis varicose

        regulate hydraeduct in range beneath Chelsea Memorial Hosp.

[1973]

Viva

for Francis L. Sweeney S.J.

Drag them out of their places,
for they block the progress of our lives, our times,
drag them out of their graves,
even if they were our parents,
for they barricade the streets of our protest, our loves;

contaminate afternoons with lanterns from poems
by questions of industry and idleness,
to swipe the mystery of storms and floods
through a stare of smug aristocracy.

Even though revolutionary epics have survived
they remain at the bottom gates
holding posts to poison the flows of experiment.

Keep fires down low to protect error, challenging uses
of light and worship, unless it be one
of trite conformity to their texts.
Encourge poverty by their avoidance
of the problems from our weird needs

That they have refused to consider
Except in terms of bare hospitality or prison
Yes, days are long they have judged
Fruitless and rewards sweet they reject
To be worthless. The nights have come that
They retire early; yes drag them out of their places
For they breed death and young graves, heartless despair
Stealing beneath bosoms to fester automatically in leeches
As enormous tumours out from the poverty of their lusts.

[1973]

Approaching the Oscars

Scotland Yard has been like a father to me. It grew me and nourished me and clothed me and housed me. Scotland Yard provides the physical and mental example for my youth and future. It defends me against my enemies, entrusting myself as sterling pattern for the future generation in the theatre and literature, teaching me the hallowed tomes in fields becoming a man gifted with the largest amount of wealth on the face of the earth.

First painting:

As a citizen of the United States, remembering Gilbert Stuart's portraits of George and Martha Washington in the Museum of Fine Arts, in my home town, Boston; then John Singer Sargent's large canvases of women or young girls, waiting in foyers for their father to return; before framed commissions for ladies at home; or of course the model for society's image: Mrs. John Gardner at her Fenway Court, where she hangs in gold and black, with white pearls about her hips; a challenge to the eye to forget.

These are what I remember from youth; and of course the great Francisco de Goya in Spain, with his enormous black-bosomed buddies, his cloak and shoulder obsessions; his need for flesh tones; his flashing dark eyes, his chocolate walk, as I recollect from marriage.

The bride books of photography seem vivid. Those cathedral-long mantillas of exquisite lace; the blue eyes of Provence, the picture books of Sir Cyril Connolly and Jerome Lerbe *Les Pavillons* with our perfect hundreds of year-old *châteaux et chaumières*, too much to expect a return from them, of the ball-gowns and heel-trains on marble terraces. Still the strain goes on, as Scotland Yard knows.

The deep-well basins, the stone-railings, intrinsic filigree and perhaps stolen Roman copies from the Renaissance pillage of Rome. Too much how little goes over the years, as the drowned fools of verse might say, in trance and eerie spell.

The quaint superstitions of theatrical folk haunt queer ruminations in poets' theatre productions of Richard Brinsley Sheridan's *The School for Scandal*, or Richard Strauss' *Der Rosenkavalier*, the semi-authentic designs ignored in production, only Scotland Yard could produce, in Hanover Square, Picadilly XVI, betrayed by the hunger of Hungarian troops in disease.

Prose Scotland Yard knows: Sherwood Anderson's *Mid American Chants*; Ernest Hemingway's *To Hell And Back* or Edgar

Allan Poe's *The Raven*, too scary to keep out of bedlam.

The other authors mentioned by either one of my employed supports are:

Rex Reed	Howard Schulman
Carl Jung	Truman Capote
William Blake	Tennessee Williams
Alex Trocchi	Allen Ginsberg
Charles Olson	John Milton

That's as far as my education in the field of literature went from the ever-faithful female impersonators who supposedly manage funds under the names of Governor John Connolly, Secretary to the Treasury of the United States of America and his broker Dominick and Dominick in this state.

Of course, one must be patient. My education went further from an escape of their tutelage; indoctrinated as it is to hospital; school; prison and church, where their habits are known and recorded under the above names.

Thirty years seem small in the above practice. Thirty years even less, when one keeps chastity, refusal and heroic vision against the indulgences found through histrionic imitations. As an experienced actor behind the footlights without knowledge of extensive William Shakespeare; *A Midsummer Night's Tale; Othello; The Merchant of Venice; Romeo and Juliet; Hamlet; Lady MacBeth* and *The Taming of the Shrew*, I found him exciting, scintillating, and profitable. The same with George Bernard Shaw, *Caesar and Cleopatra; Pygmalion;* even the work of Eugene O'Neill, badly enacted captured this audience: *The Hairy Ape; Moon Over The Caribees; Desire Under The Elms; A Moon For The Misbegotten, More Stately Mansions* continue to hold spellbound experimental researches under Scotland Yard's guidance, as does John Millington Synge's *Riders To The Sea* and Diedre of The Many Sorrows.

There are many theatrical voyeurs here in America. Many profiteers, harassing the writer and his audience. I cannot remember the transient pilgrimages to the St. James or The Wilbur for Jean Giraudoux or Christopher Fry, to the Sanders Theatre for Thomas Eliot or to the Colonial for his *The Confidential Clerk*.

Frauds out west prohibit release from home duties. The Drury Lane, as myself with Carol Channing knows keeps every treason in its archives. Without Oscar Wilde's *The Ballad of Reading Gaol*, or his *De Profundis*, I would never have imagined the horrors of prison or theology.

Cafes, restaurants, hotels in the humor of *Vile Bodies*, *The Invert*, Kay Thompson; or histories as concocted from the pens of Brooks Adams and Carl Sandburg keep some chastisement from too plentiful a budget. To do a diary in the form of love an event we best know out of our saints who too often recollect instead of correct their inner chaos. The minor operas of Gilbert and Sullivan, W. S. Maugham, F. Fitzgerald and Leo Frobenius tesify adequately the rewards of duty.

What else does Scotland Yard do for me? Or has done. It answers my phone. It speaks in foreign languages. It deceives me. It obeys civil law. It treats me when I prove it to myself that I am worthy of respect. It rejects attitudes of sociology or classicism, found through Homer Confucius or Jesus.

Dance, mais oui, by all means beneath these low-hanging beams in a lamp-lit room, teaching one another the arts of grace and courtesy, simplicity and benignity, treachery and hostility. Who could ask for more. Tricia or Dwight David Eisenhower, Junior. No, they are enough. They take me to the movies. Treat me to midnight capers. Pepper my newspapers with photography and antecdotes. And provide plentiful avenues for entertainment and exercise.

I walk alone, because to tell you the truth I like it. I talk whenever I can since that is part of my ambition. Finally with Scotland Yard ever present, touring myself as United States Ambassador to the United Nations, I keep only goodness out of sincerity, the face of records they provide to hear my work, as Bob Dylan, Paul McCartney, Billie Holiday, Libby Holman, or Gloria Swanson, including Frank Sinatra and Peggy Lee.

You see, artistry is not confined to the written word or motion-picture screen. Without either art under the aegis of David Griffith, Edouard Daguerre, Henry James and Fyodor Dostoevsky, I wonder where I would be. Surely far removed from income or hospitality. I need both of these. Need them more than church or religion, but not more than fresh air, sunshine and blue skies.

How we hope for the moonlit beaches, the steamship luxury, the private airplanes, and the star studios found this year at Culver City. It's got to be sober; it's got to be legal; it's got to be conscious and dignified.

Scotland Yard agrees in toto.

Mrs. Greer Fogelson, Esq.

[1973]

To My Chicago Friends and Publishers

It's about time I made myself clear, as to the real thrill last month
At the West End Cafe through cinema as related to verse arouses,
At a question from Charles Schub for bringing movie reviews onto
The stage, as addresses to both the reception for the film and an
Art of poetry; wherein personalities, two of whom keep in mind,
Upon passages of years: April 5th, last evening Miss Bette Davis
Celebrated on state of Boston's Symphony Hall 66 years thorough
training within audience reaction; by short selections of perhaps
a dozen theatrical masterpieces before a stunning personal appearance, in black and diamonds, microphone, dollied birthday
cake, bouquets of flowers, gold box; Just think, 66 years in the
theatre, 66 years of human living flesh and blood, against the
onslaught of time, ravages of inhuman war, disease, famine and
death. 60 years, a visionary magnet to millions in attributes of
suffering attainment, before this templed shrine of purity goodness,
and rankling, blubbery humour. I have loved Bette Davis, always,
ever since I was a little boy, and able to be old enough to go to
the movies, seeing her in my favorite scenario of them all, *Mr.
Skeffington*, alone I believed, at the time, but unescorted to adult
mores. Sincerely ten years old glad of it. As she, poor, dear grand
old Fanny gladdens 3000 patrons of an actress's life within the past
24 hours.

She was well-made up, could bow and swoop, curtsy, saunter,
sway, stoop and bend, shiver from excitement, constrain those
thundering ovations, amuse and fence usher-proctered inquiries
along different quarters, amid orchestra, levels first and second
balconies, the former where I sat, more than quite content, passed
nearly more the better part of serenest afternoon's anticipation, in
the new wing of Copley's Public Library, scanning *Leave Her To
Heaven, Anna St. Ives, Name and Address, Beyond Points of
Originated Death.*

I choose to view Miss Davis, informed of her appearance in
comparison to a personality accoladed spectacularly via celluloid
preservation; La Bouche, *Femme du Shanghai*, none other than the
notorious Rita Hayworth (Marghaeirita) Judson Welles Khan
Haymes Hill, nee Casino. Tuesday this glorious 1st and last wks.
becoming March and April.

Quantity and style are different. Rita is no pint-size. She is
strawberry blonde, while Ruth, nee Davis Farnsworth (Ms. Har-
mon Oscar Nelson) Sherry Merrill a born, natural, flaxen-haired

blonde, "mousey-colored" as might have described it to me, through my mother, of the above appellatives. Conceived like-wise, simply fair-haired Anglo-Saxon, I per chance forbear proceed embark upon a parallel description, as analysis upon them in the vein of double poetraits, viz. non-identical faces.

Golden, glimmery, shining, the former Ms. Hill sashayed through an Orson Welles production of high, dramatic note, in the building bearing his name, over Cambridge for a revival of what I believed was known a Frank Norris novel, publsh. *Shanghai.* Screenplay Sherwood King, *If I Die Before I Wake*

> "And as long as we may have   I'll never forget her.
> to go on living /   Maybe I'll die trying."

[1974]

Voce

Art, classical spontaneity.
Inspiration of millions.

My childhood's memory David
In his wheel-chair from the senior prom

At Harvard, where ivy seats of learning could
Have provided better vagony such in capacity

Who was responsible for the stroke
In the swing-time of Saint Adele, blessed sister

Poetry remains such taste of one man for his other
through cinema, opera upon bards from Theatre

Where this leopard remembers His maker
Mother, and serial number date versifier.

Au courant celebrator inform and Robert's con-
Tent constant reminder Genius surrenders not

For monetary, neither momentary pleasure;
Gnawing away particular greed that Queen Gloria

Delaunay surrenders in peculiar memory, sotto
Her maker, master, mentor survives successor

[1974]

178

My Darling Father and son

to Terry Southern

Boy, who raised me, from Hollywood to
New York, Hal's father, nourishing

Art, as if it were city goods,
namely currency found out West

from Treasury to banking firms.
Likewise Hal's son and darling god.

Leopard after my own heart's blood,
returns this Evening as genius

in person to spur the pen and mind
of Hal, myself and California sun

Shine red dirt-earth marijuana
in face of false arrests and Lila's

Robert Mitchum, Hitchcock's *Cape of
Fear; Kiss of Death*, white cargoes Ton-

Delayo lives. Hedy's John Loder.
Joe Southern; Joe Boarder priest.

[1974]

The Future

without death, resurrection only regeneration
leaves no question literary remains gross nation.

If you only take care of yourself, your country will take care
of you, dearest selection of all races, any stipulation.

Doorknobs remain brass, despite golden valuation
outside the city, or within its private stations,

over vast condotteries; they go any which
way the wind blows, Trying to guide us as bitch

40 years less coffin imitation *de vie*, medication,
outside prescription's law, an omission

I made, many times myself, as a youth running narcotics, under the impression a good turn

for my friends would yield creedence, an experience
necessary, in their faces belying anything else

except drugs' betrayal, smacking dead lips this
Evening, beside the bennies, the cotton's, the hypo's kiss.

[1974]

Anatomy

worked over, as a long thin line of paltriness before my own very
thine eyes
in defense of national shrines, as a test of mental alacrity
when the halcyon days tide abreast, retreating tender
remonstrances
between summer and autumn's holocaust apart allegianced far
separated nocturnes;
against taxing programs foisted repetitiously foreign swindle and
sorry sabotage
that those who dare to listen have responded, and shall respond
in truths our
patriotic sons and their minions attentive liberty respect

Against the challenges of bigotry and bigamism
duly resurrect before your ears the race of principles.

no man shall go unheeded when he reports his hideousness

to his hearers; the visage of which minions likewise as sell
expect noted.
Unasian purposes traced before your eyes, as suprises the-
oreticians mock
sovereign permissive textualness.

In sufficient verdiction as manufacture ineffectualness
entertains
indigeousness enactment's wholeheartedly

forbidden to smaller fortunes or larger leagues.
In other words, when you walk in fear of labor, or chase
down tenement graft

I am Tenth Walker upon Windy Towers, I am married to Saint
Francis Sienna

I come by train; in caravans up to date thousands of battered
homesteads

through his kisses as 12s into twenties wend gracious boulevards
courting

181

chastity from his killing traffic.

God what has spoken against his mark, his mail, his message?

Meditate willfully thy master, as called phones delay this missives.

The shrines of Toledo speak his goodness, sepulchres of Jersey
rent twin tuxedos, aghast when twelve
lords castigate Chicago, two decades ago.
Tribes of the

Iroquois impersonated but expelled away due cargo.

[1974]

182

Cultural Affairs in Boston

I. He Cannot Take Any Credit For This One

A 300,000 solid bloc of citizens relate specific to noblesse oblige, by consternation outgoingly beside overall conveyance, as *materia duomo* to your editor's request for alleviating work: labor should be an indiscreet thing, assuming the subtlety of its community in the face of "landlord's" sine fear inhabitors, the working girl, without question imposition. If credibility is the initial factor, the unearthing of one's position could indicate ulterior evidence of pertinence approaching truth. I like to hazard the guaranty a behavior-involvement would reduce the withholding circumstances, attributable to man's position in society. For my servants, after all, the working man is not a dual-motivated hypothesis. Outre-contradictionedly to employ yourself towards in words, otherwise another human person: thus, not work, but repetitiously as a document, that one cannot, or should not be conceived independent, is sagacious.

II.

Believe me, you can be nobody else, but who you are. I have known many who tried; in service to Our Lord: not as a hypocrite, enjambement, a typical example being: that man can stand just so much exhumation: Borgias non-exempt, examination. I take great delight, in writing, preparing against anxiety. Hopeful the terms of two decades promote applicability in a quaint respect for native INNS, upperworld restoration against fancy prices and chamber attitudes. Experiencing *Fashion*, conversely atop my building, where mercy like Ty McDonnell, McConnell, in the lead of McAlpin-Herald Sqe: reservations notwithstanding displayed last winter his treasure of that duo experience. Somewhat similarly to the natural lobby for Fernanda's Park Square Complex. Come rain or shine, staying out for a night. Remember the *Luxor*!? And those Finnish baths, unmentionably *The Continental*, for abduction to Luise Workers, over 1st Ave; and 20th Street, single Fortnight Free, Involuntarily. Heartbreakingly it was not Cairo, only stolen from there. Vide: MIAMI BEACHES *Albion*. A.P.

III. Male Prostitution Out Of Miami Beach Into The
Mountains Of Las Vegas

What do I have next door?
Where do you think they're headed for, now.

Dennis, James und Hector.

2 days
North, and west Welles Chicago

through panteraidens and E. Sr. Athens

them's the Hayworth legs, alright,
I wish I could afford it,

a pair
and the outlaw shorn

    of his
            studio sheepskein

            dame Rona,

You do not o.o. wrk. except when talking to a woman.

Go weird, asking do you got any extra matches on you?

    address to officer:
        your help

IV.

As a 20 or 30 year old, to get in town was a supreme taste of la
rue before Beacon Street's Town House and thusly grow up, as a
mental addict of boulevardier, nearby the park and commons. How
I treasure those evenings near the rialto top-price admissions
hereafter Know priorly the Carnival's Pilgrim, exploded by those
people who are standing in the way of this piece. Destroy the
evidence, of course. Of the Holiday *Inn* and *The Chelsea*. ALBERT,
please remember how happy we were in the search for rooms.

Earnestly only that, doggedly enroute Paris, Holland, Vienna, London and T.O.S.T. Irvington R.F.M. Do you think, p.e. Nico mite recall sounding Sonesta, platinum, befurred & p.a.c.p. Electric *Cirque*. You can be sure THE LOVER'S CHAUFFEUR does. I have always written well, re Commodore, Commander, Cambridge, witness this walk home in anonymous leif-motif. CORANDEL Backstairs Queen Pantry

If you feel demoralized and
don't know why exactly, could
it be the cutlasses from old
assassins remonstrate diebold
headlines, *There are Catholics*
in California or *I'm not Dishonest*
sourdough breadlines overshadowy patios,
wealthy extortionists, two guillotines rack
youth and M.P. set of their felonious beat pack
Boyscouts from Croupiers on Van Ness Caterpaults
supplant national allegiance as evidence that
"The March of Siamese Children" imitate
by celluloid Norton Union actual feats
oh those rainy Hearst verandahs, cupola weather vanitate
Dear Surplus Harewood Court has gilt lobby and a glass
      mirror, in temper to
steel, besides swank living room in tune to early
      Thanksgiving alloy
and silk sitting room for our Virgin Mary, with sweet
      parlor
aside for Rose? Kennedy to mourn with Fre. Peyton
      Spencerboy.

      Louisiana   JOHN J. Wieners

[1974]

185

Sexual facts are tiring, too

Ignorance, seduction
There is a certain titillation / that surrounds the air, / where you
                                                                    live
The movement of hips past the car window
The relentless search for release

in cabaret, on the riverbank

The group of homosexuals invades the city.
They are decimated by time, alcohol

and each is left with his own condition

The green scarf from the cabinet door
provokes self-extension.

Ascertain stimulation from living in the city,
seeing the beautiful women,
hearing the drums start in the early afternoon

[1974]

There are very important minutes

That time, upon waking, or during Sunday evening shopping rush hours in disguises cast off for the bettering, overall true pitch for public welfare wherein plural man forced to undergo committed decisions undertakes his heart's purposed passion despite the amassed face from mutilated multitudes Goodnes has nothing, or conversely, something to with it being evaluated either in want or next to everything. When incurred risking censure, from available, alas and to avail extant allowances forecloses our practical advices in these albeit said quarters down; hankering patent places of apt heartiness open handedness before trusty preferentials unto aimless conviviality withal comely as to hasty and cautioned retreat less contradicting ledgermain any former earliers detachments, say, in that a forefront where subsidy done thoroughly sizeable proportioned dog-sledding, seizing the most of a good opportunity betters their person al homily.

The flowered prints of a skirt; responsive carnet *de Mode*; in other words suggestive embellishment to a hum-drum anonymous implicit succinctness; of conduct in conscience.

Returning from the theatre, if it is only a re-run in the Orson Welles Triple Cinema Complex, after seeing ourselves upon the screeners' makeshift additions and never absent heretofore detractions to the subsidized pointing up humble apologies towards best correct motive reactionary super star rysdom, apropos legislative decorum where nevertheless apathetic notions hold pre-eminence, as to what platinum blondes are really upto, in grabbing men into toolboxes, purring slyly running bourbons, torchily and unduly on all fronts, releasing trophies. There is something about Elpenor losing his mast helm to lost backstreet grip from Baby Bee-Bea's tongue, that is a plugged nickel don't fit the slot or oilt monthly dames take the edge off Dick's pursuance to bedroom drips up in strumpet's water-closet.

[1975]

Home Surgery at Merchant Marine

To get your degree, in lavender
follow after me, Norris dental provider

forty-year old eyes, legs university
plush Frederick Single bow C

a tiny cupid's safety
twenty less five

times a $15 single
room on Scott Street

with Dicky. Oh dear Pile
what's the difference between

a pocketful of silver coins
and three or four hundred dollars

man Rodgers, please remember to keep
Mass turf my Dghtr's feet

never toucht the ground
Smiley son's balls are kept

between another man's thighs.
Play both sides of the street

Forever Walley prefers First cognative
formal Ace Pente, hyphen colon in honorife

from Jimmy Witherspoon, Cliff
Jordan & those all-night discs.

[1975]

I've Lived Here Longer than Anybody Else
and I Know Where Everything Is

Just think, also I've lived here
all through two years, over sixteen months
  with a broken bathroom window
and not one man has ever made even the
  slightest attempt to crawl through it.

  Don't worry, I'm not asking for trouble
  and surely not looking for it, yet
    my good luck amazes me. Even still don't let them
      stand in your way, reading conducts gets grades the mind.

You see, I broke it myself, deciphered Steves locked
myself out one Sunday afternoon, I think it was
and my neighbor let me crawl up the fire escape
  through his. I know how cruel and mean some people can be.
    Never mind, things go well, and I've progressed from a small
                                           flat
    over *The Lower Depths*, in keeping with your destiny, as the
                                       Mother
  of God. Yes, I call my imaginary Lover, god, my husband, my
                                      only wish
  now is to become a woman, for all of them, an Empress upon
                                  your Eastern shore.

[1975]

189

Pest

I live in a flop
half-looped,
blood stains on skirt
nor chained to a bed,

a phantom kiss for company
communicating archly
by Anne the terror of
tenement tragedy.

Passers-by perhaps
recognize the face
to promenade in
chance their glance

populates disbarred midnight.

[c. 1975]

"Twenty Years"

Twenty years. Just think, twenty years seem a long time. Twenty years in prison is not the same thing, as living on the border fringes of the underworld, and meeting, always meeting for a short time, persons who were sent up for a short time.

If he were prince, or the lordliest man on earth, or the richest one, as he was prone to employ himself, he would not do any different than the law had already wreaked. He, Frank B. Chadloner, with only a Doctor of Laws degree, could see that the law was for the strong, not the weak. It was designed to protect the enormously powerful, and even he, with only honorary doctorate could see the weak must never be allowed to sift through a wealthy figure's person. He must be locked up.

The statutes, commandments, amendements were constitued by absolute monarchs.

Inclusion of Prince Charles Speech

Of course, if you suffer any loss of liberty, or threatened loss, you know what a generation of twenty years in losses might add up to. The clean breaths, fresh air

Now Prince of Charles speech

[1976]

"I don't have a thought in my head"

I don't have a thought in my head, silent-screen version
or a friend in the form of devotional orders, across corporation
drawing board because then New England Navy department city
relinquishes commanding maritime-shore leave officers to foreign
ports hinterlands, without compunction leashing our expenses
formerly better accounts. How stands it to reason therefore that
testament that all ashore that's going ashore undoes question marks
when—consideration savors of savvy savoir-faire? One wouldn't
go so far as to say, the waves predispose assignment, in the face
of screentests, that is to say, one knows when a big boat is home,
thereby nearing land, that the wind from his sails smacks apartment suite curtain shades, in just a certain way, headed out of in,
familiarly as journey-man over and above the call of duty, he has
forgotten his particularity on board, above a generalization upon
a voyage, only that the regulars at home, spy because shore-sprit,
beckon ahoy in the mast-head, over coming ennui and shipman-
shape their duty's expected. Thus one pays through proverbial
brown noses, for murder, off hands project zero no, for cellular star-
dom, even less for midnight cavortings akin Carnegie Esplanade
Shell mayhem but over to East Coast halcyon carriage hostels, for
all suggestion delicate zephyrs preserved in juxtaposition that
Russia puts anchorage into tranquil belfry harbor, just yesterday
aft. when sunset depict the poker hand trade.

[August 14, 1975]

Fifteen Minutes in a Cheap Hotel

We enjoy poverty more than wealth.
With Louis B. Mayer, real well
Especially going to a Holiday Inn
in the morning, dangerously for coffee.

And Molly Goldberg's love-child, at home.

I'm asking you, when a woman looks over her left

shoulder, is she storm-Troopering early,
like I never made the Boy Scouts.

Too masculine, due to a house of ill-repute,

run by Mary McCarthy anti-climax.

How dumb can you get, with a full set of teeth?

[1975]

Moira

who lights a kerosene lamp in her bungalow
as her "husband" shoves 800,000 dollars below
his teats to provide for society's shadow

shopping for pickles along the row
while creole bands open their mouths to blow
jazz over the radio, a black velvet bow

around her brow, as sign she is Krakow
from Chinese dynasty to Sussex meadow,
a mistinguett in London's Soho snow.

[1975]

194

The Book and the Lamp

Aida

The book, *Homolibre* basalt
and the Lamp that didn't light
without a switch: Juanita Hall
like that department store
outside of Amherst's airefield strip.
psychologues *en français bohèmes*

Hidden away in the librarian poet's corner
and latin men smooching on the cover,
Two guys, semi-sepia's bitch.

—Spanish Mexicale, as Cleopatran quest,
are you Catholic La Gioconda:
some kind of snake dancer's alley officer search
rummager what does one ex-cathedra think of Algren's
                                    bare-chested biceps
                          Bert's arches question pugilist
funnys sine columban Vatican Lisa prelude.

[1976]

After you go in the dark room

To Steve Jonas

I know what you're using me for
measuring furs up to these elbows
to get the laugh on the bar-flies around Sporter's
and to get back at your hoity-toity friends

sorta when crashing your pearls aways
and to get my husband's hands around your throat,
after I've pressed the button to tell him
you're not charging;

  spill the last word Mata, over Hanoi Hanna
so you can turn your back on Tokyo Iva,

and look the German Axis square in the eye,
backward picking up Brocades' hem
then douse the lights, ah
well, . . . the moon comes up—.

[1976]

196

Upon Central Ave and Milton
By Irene Dunne

Some women go abroad just to his downstairs. To the clinics, the Sanitoriums "to get their mind toned up," against the frauds of bag waitresses, pursuing beer heiresses' dowries; as in the case of Mildred "Eilars." Short-term bank withdrawals at the point of a sawed-off hope. Ladies in retirement suppose Mildred the toast for their morning coffee, when this writer assumes her deportation lends attitudes *de hauteur contre* security and spacious recompense. Pay-offs never mean more than popular aversion. And the Voice of America portends to deprive Ms. "Eilars" of those liberties others as Mickey Mouse and garbled mobsters frequently regret to report.

This evening reading of the bowdlerization against my former places of residence I realize that thousands of United States, and foreign currency have been seized to cover losses by those *b a g* gun-molls against early work of mine in the 1940's for WWD, viz pp. *One, Eighteen* and *ten.*

It's suicidal to go on until those lost females return who know the score of these hopeless pretenses to honest money. My mother worked 39 years to educate me against dishonesty. No son or radio interpreter along announcements pertaining to these Fourth decade Facts should relinquish his or her inherited rights to their savored dowries while the meaningless Cat and Mouse game of purposeless "cops" or "robbers" multiply.

Samuel Feinberg
Paul Hannenberg
Dolores Guinness

[1976]

Mrs. Francis Griffith

"night, that last month of the last"

night, that last month of the last
year's spring to hasten lovely Lenore's
grave. With his taped monologue truth
to him, a sexual deviate known as Walter
but occasionally epicurean enough
called Scott, he begged for release
from incarceration out of State
punishment. I rang for a gun
from a friend, as he thought it
would prove tricky to effect such
privilege. Lenore heard this
and collapsed, dying in Pa's

[1976]

Pod's Acre

Since 1969, I have seen over 4,000 attractive pulchritudinous shapely, young artistic Ladies performing, in various tasks about their familiar occupations. Respecting talent, coming into a broader relation vitally for 33 solid years, has left me undivided and undiminished in as to what they declare the minor, portion, majorally speaking, with what the average male in his 5 year residence around your city would recover.

It keeps active mental alert, faculties in seeing to these generous tasks set down by way of ordinate authorizations demeaned, or deployed throughout large, partial businesses.

Could you hazard a glance, traipsing one end of Tremont to the other out front the Bavarian park, their calm and industrious indolence legalize sanctification for the wayward office attaining youth.

Canon, granite steps, antique stairways, starless iron railings, your wonderful arms and proud, grassy boughs specify the throbbing passion peters full uncovering chastitise.

It does little for a man to live alone, but I do it.

Glad to sneak a look now and then, at the opposite sex. When applause dictates attendance, we in the role of bachelorhood will be there, shelling our peas into half of God's blossoming orchard.

[1976]

"The party that no one came to"

The party that no one came to
Victory, but what about triumph
ah, an entry we laugh to remember.

[1976]

What a Poet Is For...

It's a dangerous racket,
being regarded as a religious object,
and it is a racket, if you
don't admit to it.

                    Reign.

[1976]

Doll

How many loves had I
in young boy's bed,
at Humarock, or Provincetown's
Cape Cod, under sweating summer sun,

after Land's End, before their interruption.
How many loves had I?

in discourse by firelight, after highballs
to records of Marlene Dietrich and Cole Porter,
how many loves had I?

in Swampscott flat, or Beacon Hill house,
Beacon Street garage or Fiedler overpass,
how many loves had I?

How many loves, in Annandale
before payment or threat, in the Public Gardens
or Fifth Avenue park, how many loves—

None, none, none at all.

[1976]

Pull

Oh, holy most blessed
to support us over or upto almost these
past eight years, since

you revealed my identity
in which guise, oh almighty one
even beloved

never to starve, let alone endure
obscurity as Verdi would
have known the Lateran

pact without His name

This is just an excuse to exercise my
handwriting. I'm saying my handwriter
lives longer on my part, as Paul
Andrews; as the boy who goes to the
Dentist with me, as the darling Higgin-

B   O   T   H   A   M

out of Bellevue into Sugar Babies.

                              Up-side Down.

Jesuits in mufti, on the way
to blowing George Saintsbury
their founder

meet up logues, as old ladies
walking animals
hence animal skirts

A birthday comes but once a year.
When you're 46, it lasts all your life.
There is no more cognizance due to

Kremlin neighbors, inhabiting Burns.

Imitatio Christi

[January 6, 1980]

For a Cover of *Art News*

Are you still among the living?
                out there in California, Tatiana
                                Alexander

With the Seattle Art Gallery. 1959
                from that small hotel bed 1 am
                                weight

of young lips.

[1985]

The Fountainhead

                        for Barbara Stanwyck

To see the lights come on in Los Angeles, where
You're looking at the best of New York multi-millionaires;
But it's not everyday you can sit in a chair
And see it from a $240 room; higher than imperturbable and
                                                ancient
these sidewalks, where we presume only female impersonators
                                                view
wondrous exclamities in the direction of a post-moderne middle
                                                class"

[1985]

Charity Balls

I had a fellowship, but lived poorly
On slices of pizza.
Later, a career of washing lettuce;
but I have always been the same.
It's a question of acquiring a mastery of tone
Beneath the crystal chandeliers and champagne
on a glass table top.
At the age of five I thought Scarlett O'Hara
a fictional character. It was not until
The age of forty-eight I knew she was real.
Old clothes and bedroom slippers and a scarf
Wrapped around her head
In low cost tenement housing.
She began talking about my writing
And her sex life.
I'm curt by nature and dolorous.
But I knew if I worked hard I'd eventually make it.

[October 2, 1985]

Index of Titles and First Lines

Printed August 1988 in Santa Barbara &
Ann Arbor for the Black Sparrow Press by
Graham Mackintosh & Edwards Brothers, Inc.
Design by Barbara Martin. This edition
is published in paper wrappers; there are
400 cloth trade copies; & 226 hardcover
copies have been handbound in boards by
Earle Gray & are signed by John Wieners,
Robert Creeley & Raymond Foye.

John Wieners was born in Milton, Mass. in 1934 and received his A.B. from Boston College in 1954. He studied at Black Mountain College under Charles Olson and Robert Duncan from 1955 to 1956. He returned to Boston where he brought out three issues of a literary magazine, *Measure*, over the next several years. From 1958 to 1960 he lived in San Francisco, and was an active participant in the San Francisco Poetry Renaissance. He returned to Boston in 1960, and divided his time between there and New York City, over the next five years. In 1965 he enrolled in the Graduate Program of the State University of New York at Buffalo, and worked as a teaching fellow. He has worked as an actor and stage manager at the Poet's Theatre, Cambridge, and has had three of his plays performed at the Judson Poet's Theater, N.Y. Since 1970 he has lived and worked in Boston, where he has been active in publishing and education cooperatives, political action committees, and the gay liberation movement.

Raymond Foye was born in Lowell, Mass., in 1957, and studied at the San Francisco Art Institute. He has worked as a free lance editor for City Lights Books, New Directions, Petersburg Press and Alfred A. Knopf. He is currently publisher of Raymond Foye Editions, New York, devoted to poet/painter collaborations, and co-publisher (with Francesco Clemente) of Hanuman Books. He is the editor of a previous collection of John Wieners' work, *Selected Poems: 1958–1984*, published in 1986 by Black Sparrow Press.